"... This book is a must read for every Christian who is genuine about being a Christ follower today."

Neville Wight, former senior pastor,
Carnegie COC, Australia

"If your favorite place is the couch, with TV remote in hand, do not read this book; Hon's down to earth exposition of the Revelation will be a danger to your peace of mind. Hon shows that God's plans for the future do not involve Christians sitting comfortably in the corporate box watching the game with free coke and hot dogs. In fact, it seems that God expects us to be sweating it out on the playing field, wearing His team colors. This book will assist anyone wanting to be a useful player on God's team as it provides motivation, an understanding of what the goals are and will help you to identify and overcome the opposition."

David Hobson, Managing Director,
Emtivac Engineering Pty. Ltd.

"Pastor Hon Hoh has written an eminently readable study on Revelation. He writes with a pastoral heart, seeking to communicate the Apocalypse plainly and simply. Herein lies his great contribution to this often misunderstood book. Study questions at the end of each chapter help readers to contextualize and apply what they learned. I highly recommend it."

Mark Lim, International Pastor,
Crossway Baptist Church, Victoria, Australia

"I had the privilege of sharing in ministry with Hon Hoh at the Clayton Church of Christ Fellowship. During those years I came to appreciate Hon's fresh insight, clear understanding and skilled handling of the Scriptures in his preaching and teaching. Hon's passion for God and commitment to His Word continues to be lived out as Pastor, Director of Living Impact Ministries and now as an author. I am sure you will enjoy his insights, practical application and be assisted in gaining a clearer understanding of the Book of Revelation as he presents them in *Risen Lamb - Empowered Saints*."

"Clear, straight forward, balanced across the whole of Scripture. An 'eye opener' to our progress towards the great day of the Lord's return. Deeply thought provoking, personally challenging, yet very exciting as Hon has unfolded many of the confusing aspects of the Revelation into practical principles … A must for any home group study."

"*Risen Lamb, Empowered Saints* is an excellent and practical book … for our generation. It … focuses on the very reason that Jesus had for His revelation — to change us into His image and spiritually prepare us for all that He has in store for us. This book assists the reader to prepare for His return … regardless of when or how or whatever that might happen. This is a valuable book … and for the first time, provides an overall view of the 'forest' and its grandeur, rather than a detailed look at each individual 'tree.' "

"Excellent, interesting, helpful, readable. Hon Hoh has opened windows of information for any student of the Bible."

"While written as a series of sermons, both Christians and non-Christians alike can take a step closer to grasping the true message of Revelation. Whether read as a daily devotional or a book, *Risen Lamb, Empowered Saints* takes us beyond the graphics so prevalent in the most relevant Book of the new millennium."

"Pastor Hon's approach is fresh, passionate, and very personal. He brings the book of Revelation back to where it belongs ... in our hearts."

Dr. Iwan Tumewa, founding chairman,
Young Entrepreneur's Organization Indonesia,
Indonesian Entrepreneur Development Foundation

"Hon Hoh has been a good friend of mine for the past 20 years ... . He walks closely with the Lord, therefore, intimacy with God is real to Hon, and as he listens to the Lord, so he has revelation knowledge to impart to his readers!"

Merrilyn Teague, Pastor of the Austral Asian Christian Church,
Adelaide, South Australia

"Whenever I read this book or listen to Hon preach on the book of Revelation, I pray that more people will have the chance to read or hear it. I feel that God speaks to me through it."

Fred Gong, Manager,
Burwood Ozi Tek Computers, Victoria, Australia

"This book should meet a real need in the Christian community where there is so much fear, misconception and confusion about Revelation and so many mental and spiritual blocks to people studying it. Its pastoral approach is just what is needed and is compatible with the purpose for which Jesus gave us this vision. The small, nonthreatening size is a plus too. Hon Hoh has managed to condense the main themes and interpretations of symbols into relatively few words and do it intelligibly. I think Hon has done a great job, been faithful to biblical principles of interpretation, applied the message relevantly to the contemporary situation yet avoided the temptation to speculate or sensationalize."

Dr. Keith Hinton, Director of Postgraduate Studies,
Bible College of Victoria, Australia

LIVING IMPACT

*Releasing resources
for strategic ministry impact.*

Living Impact Inc. is a nondenominational Christian ministry reaching the most unreached nations of the world in a region known as the 10/40 Window.

You can participate with us in seven ways

A. Sponsor an indigenous worker
For a small amount each month you can help release an indigenous church planter into the neediest parts of the world. All sponsorship funds go to the field. Nothing is taken for administration.

B. Intercede for Living Impact
Intercessors receive monthly prayer notes via email.

C. Contribute to a special need
Special needs and projects are listed on our website.

D. Donate an offering
Assist our essential operational costs.

E. Go with us on short term missions

F. Read our newsletter
Living Impact News is published quarterly.

G. Give a copy of this book to your friends
Proceeds will assist in this ministry.

If you would like a brochure, please write to:

Living Impact
15 Jacob Drive
Rowville, Victoria 3178
Australia

www.livingimpact.org

contact@livingimpact.org

Risen Lamb, Empowered Saints

The Book of Revelation Made Easy

---

by

Hon S. Hoh

Fairmont Books is a ministry of The McDougal Foundation, Inc., a Maryland nonprofit corporation dedicated to spreading the Gospel of the Lord Jesus Christ to as many people as possible in the shortest time possible.

Published by:

Fairmont Books
P.O. Box 3595
Hagerstown, MD 21742-3595
www.mcdougalpublishing.com

ISBN 978-1-58158-061-7

Printed in the United States of America
For Worldwide Distribution

DEDICATION

To Voon Ling — my wife and best friend — in our twelfth year of marriage.

Acknowledgments

This book would not have been possible without the involvement of three Australian churches. The first time I preached an expository series through the book of Revelation was at South Yarra Church of Christ. Little did I know at the time I would one day write a book on the Apocalypse. The second occasion was at Clayton Church of Christ Fellowship, during which I did exegesis on the Revelation for a second time as part of my preparation for the Sunday sermons. The third expository series was preached at Carnegie Church of Christ, during which I decided to write this book as part of my preparation for the messages. My sincere thanks go to all who patiently sat through the sermon series. Their positive feedback and encouragement have been most valuable.

Acknowledgment should also go to Dr. Keith Hinton, under whom I first studied the Revelation at the Bible College of Victoria. He made the book digestible, interesting and challenging. Thanks should also go to Dr. Rikki Watts, who taught me how to exegete the Bible like none other. Without the knowledge and wisdom he imparted I might not have approached the Revelation with sufficient confidence.

Finally, I would like to thank my wife, Ling, who has been my greatest supporter during this long process of preaching and writing. She is the greatest blessing God has brought into my life, and the best friend I have ever had.

Contents

Publisher's Note

In recent years, we have shied away from publishing books that deal with the details of end-time events because there are so many conflicting theories, and any such book is bound to offend someone. We came to the conclusion that it was better not to publish what brought division to the Body of Christ.

Upon review of Hon Hoh's manuscript, we felt that this is a book worthy of publication. Every reader may not agree with all of his conclusions, but he has approached the book of Revelation from a very refreshing viewpoint. He refuses to argue over the timing of end-time events, and instead, presents a very positive and challenging message to the Church. Readers can reach their own conclusions about the timing and details of particular events.

Harold McDougal
McDougal Publishing

FOREWORD

With so much current interest in issues of the future and the supernatural, a study of the Book of Revelation is timely. Its grandeur, insights and imagery have captivated readers throughout the century. In light of current events, it makes sense to take another look at this remarkable book. It is the only book in the Bible that promises blessing to those who read and heed its precepts (see Revelation 1:3).

This powerful book has also been much maligned. Its foes have relegated it to the past or the fringe, or they have discounted it as too mysterious to be understandable. Even "friends" of Revelation has mishandled its sacred script by careless date-setting of the Second Coming of Christ, endeavoring to find meaning to every minute detail, or by trying to squeeze it into every major modern event. Whether friend or foe, the promised blessing of Revelation remains deferred because people remain unsure how to handle it.

Thankfully, there is another way. In *Risen Lamb, Empowered Saints*, Hon Hoh offers an eminently readable presentation of this remarkable book. Carefully outlined, clearly written, thoughtfully analized and pastorally delivered, Hoh offers the reader a gentle, but solid, introduction to Revelation. Carefully combining current issues against the backdrop of the biblical narrative, the original Greek, with practical application for Christian living, *Risen Lamb, Empowered Saints* gives the reader a sane and solid overview, reasonable options in interpretation and, most importantly, continual application for daily Christian living. Study questions at the end of the chapter are provided to review, reinforce and re-invent, when necessary.

Whether you are new to the study of Revelation or a seasoned student, you are sure to gain insight. Prepare to be informed, challenged and blessed.

Rev. Kameel Majdali, Ph.D., Principal
Harvest Bible College
Melbourne, Australia

INTRODUCTION

In this short introduction I would like to explain why I have decided to write this book. I see the Revelation as one of the most relevant books of the Bible to our day and age. This is contrary to what many Christians think, most of whom openly state their difficulty in understanding it. I remembered preaching at a conference where a pastor freely confessed to me that he is confused about the Apocalypse. I was asking if he thought it would be useful in the future to teach a series on the Revelation. His answer was an absolute and unequivocal yes. There is a real need for Christians to understand the book.

The world has entered the third millennium. Apocalyptic speculations could possibly increase. In such times, I would like to see that Christians are able to speak confidently with their friends and colleagues regarding the book of Revelation. I would love to see the truths and perspective contained in Revelation motivate them as they have motivated me to be a more committed follower of Jesus.

I believe Christians are missing out significantly when they fail to comprehend the Revelation. This is especially so when the book was divinely inspired to be read, understood and obeyed. Wasn't that the reason John wrote it under the inspiration of the Holy Spirit? *"Blessed is the one who reads the words of this prophecy, and blessed are those who hear it and take to heart what is written in it, because the time is near"* (Revelation 1:3). I remember being invited to present an overview of the book to a home fellowship group where a member asked if it was really necessary for Christians to understand the Revelation! I do not for one moment blame Christians for not grasping or not appreciating the book. After all, I was in that situation for years and I did not value its importance simply because I could not comprehend it. But now that I grasp the simplicity of its message and the power of its perspective, I want others to share in the liberation I have experienced.

It has been quite a number of years since I first studied the book in depth, and since then I have preached it as an expository series three times at three different churches. The first was to a small inner-city church. The second was to a large suburban congregation of 500. The third was to another suburban church where I was the teaching pastor. From the feedback I have received, many people have greatly appreciated the 22-sermon series. One person wrote to me saying: "Your exposition on the book of Revelation has helped me to discover the power and the glory of our Lord Jesus Christ in the midst of hurtful, chaotic and uncertain times in this world."

My conviction is that the book of Revelation can be studied and understood without excessive speculation. It is powerful in the perspective it offers to those living at the commencement of a new century. It is highly relevant to us who live in the environmentally conscious global village. Its comprehension is absolutely necessary for Christians wanting to make a difference in a world where some of the prophecies are being and will be fulfilled. The book of Revelation is not dispensable diet for the everyday believer. It must not be relegated only to the realm of the theological seminary. It is a book for you and me.

Risen Lamb, Empowered Saints: The Book of Revelation Made Easy was written with this in mind. It is easy to understand. It is practical and applicable. You can enjoy it as a book or as a daily devotional. It can be used as a Bible study tool, as each chapter contains study and discussion questions. It was written basically as a sermon series. It is *not* a commentary. I did not write it as a theologian or an exegete. I wrote it as a pastor.

Hon S. Hoh
Rowville, Victoria, Australia

Chapter 1

THE REASON FOR REVELATION

Revelation 1:1-8, NRSV:

The revelation of Jesus Christ, which God gave him to show his servants what must soon take place; he made it known by sending his angel to his servant John, {2} who testified to the word of God and to the testimony of Jesus Christ, even to all that he saw.

{3} Blessed is the one who reads aloud the words of the prophecy, and blessed are those who hear and who keep what is written in it; for the time is near.

{4} John to the seven churches that are in Asia:

Grace to you and peace from him who is and who was and who is to come, and from the seven spirits who are before his throne, {5} and from Jesus Christ, the faithful witness, the firstborn of the dead, and the ruler of the kings of the earth.

To him who loves us and freed us from our sins by his blood, {6} and made us to be a kingdom, priests serving his God and Father, to him be glory and dominion forever and ever. Amen.

{7} Look! He is coming with the clouds; every eye will see him, even those who pierced him; and on his account all the tribes of the earth will wail.

So it is to be. Amen.

{8} "I am the Alpha and the Omega," says the Lord God, who is and who was and who is to come, the Almighty.

Introductory Remarks

"Look at the fig tree and all the trees. When they sprout leaves, you can see for yourselves and know that summer is near. Even so, when you see these things happening, you know that the kingdom of God is near." This was what Jesus

said in Luke 21:29-31 after He had taught the disciples concerning the end times. The disciples were asking, "What will be the sign that they are about to take place?" In answer to their curiosity, Jesus exhorted them to "look" and "see" that they may be prepared and not be found wanting. The church is expected by Jesus to understand the times and know what they should do as His people. In my experience I have come across some who do not want to understand the times in which they live. They seem to bury their heads in the sand and wish for the best. Jesus exhorts us to do otherwise.

What are the signs of the end? In 1994 there was a program on television entitled "Ancient Prophecies." In it the book of Revelation was quoted, together with Nostradamus, Our Lady of Fatima, St. Malachy, Edgar Cayce and others. All the secular prophecies mentioned apparently predicted cataclysmic events happening around the year 2000 or soon after it. A nuclear holocaust was to be expected, diseases would reach epidemic proportions, all marking the end of history as we have it. Well, we have passed the year 2000. Will end-time fever increase as we progress further into the new millennium? How will the events of September 11 affect our thinking? With the book of Revelation being quoted and misquoted by Christians and non-Christians alike, the questions we need to ask and answer are: "What does the Revelation really teach? What does it have to say concerning the signs of the end?" Christ called them blessed who read and obey the words of His prophetic book.

Although we are encouraged to understand the contents of Revelation, it is worth emphasizing at the outset the warning given in Revelation 22:18-19: *"I warn everyone who hears the words of the prophecy of this book: If anyone adds anything to them, God will add to him the plagues described in this book. And if anyone takes words away from this book of prophecy, God will take away from him his share in the tree of life and in the holy city, which are described in this book."* As one who writes on the book I want to be careful that I do not indulge in unhealthy speculations about it. I, for one, do not want to share in any of these plagues as described. I suspect neither do you.

Let me now offer a few important general comments. First, Revelation is without doubt one of the most relevant books in the Bible to our day. This is true for both Christians and non-Christians. We live in the early twenty-first century where millennium speculations abound and will likely increase as we progress. Recently on television was a repeat of the 1993 movie starring Demi Moore called "The Seventh Sign." As I had not watched the movie I thought I might indulge myself since I was writing on the Revelation! In line with my expectation, the film was full of unscriptural conjectures, and worst of all, verses from Revelation were regularly quoted. I thought to myself how easy it would have been for a Christian who is not familiar with the Apocalypse to be deceived or at least confused by the movie. It certainly reminded me of similar movies, such as "Omen I and II" and "The Final Conflict," in which the Antichrist was eventually killed by a special dagger. But millennium speculations are here to stay. I wonder how many thought it was the beginning of the end when Saddam Hussein took on the United States in the Gulf War in 1991. Perhaps many more have concluded that way after September 2001.

The second comment I want to make is that studying this book would mean tackling some of the megathemes of Christianity and of philosophy. Consider the following themes running through the book:

- Suffering and God's sovereignty: If God is sovereign, why is there suffering and the increase of it as the end draws near?
- Evil and political oppression: Why do they occur, and how do they relate to the Kingdom of God?
- Cosmic conflict: How does spiritual warfare work out in everyday life, and how will it intensify?
- The Second Coming: When will it happen, and will the Rapture really take place before the final tribulation?
- Eschatology: What are the signs, and how do we avoid excessive speculations while meaningfully examining the subject?
- Final Judgment and punishment: Will it really occur, or will we just be annihilated?
- The Lamb and His Gospel: In what ways are they central to our faith?
- The role of the Church: How should we then live?

My third general comment is this: Revelation is basically a pastoral letter. Yes, it is called apocalyptic literature because it deals with cataclysmic events that occur at the conclusion of the age, but it is fundamentally John's pastoral exhortation to the Church. The year was around A.D. 90 when the apostle John was in exile on the island of Patmos. John had oversight of many of the churches in Asia Minor, in particular the leading church of Ephesus. Sporadic persecutions were happening under the reign of the Roman emperor Domitian, and John wanted to encourage his churches to stand firm in the faith regardless of circumstances. In the divine miracle of inspiration, he writes the letter of Revelation under the unction of the Spirit. How did the apostle encourage his churches? What spiritual medicine did he prescribe? The remedy John offered was for them to take a long look at Jesus Christ, the risen Lamb, and a short look at their problems. This has some very practical applications for us. Are you discouraged in your situation? Perhaps the routine of life is bogging you down, or maybe you are facing some seemingly insurmountable problems. Let me encourage you to apply John's remedy to discouragement by taking a short look at your problem and a long look at God. This is what you'll find yourself doing as we journey through the book. Revelation gives us a fresh glimpse of Jesus Christ and exhorts us to look hard into the face of God.

The Journey

Perhaps it is appropriate at this point to explain briefly how I will be walking through the book. First, let me emphasize what I will not be doing. In this book I will not be giving a verse-by-verse commentary through every chapter. This is especially so in the chapters following the letters to the seven churches. If you are looking for a commentary, there are a few good ones around, for instance the one by Robert Mounce in the *New International Commentary on the New Testament* series. A shorter and less technical one is *The Message of Revelation* by Michael Wilcock.

I will also not attempt to interpret every symbol that is in Revelation. Some symbols are more important than others, and I will definitely make an attempt at interpreting the more significant ones. You can be certain that every symbol that has an important bearing on the main message of the passage will be interpreted. I will not, however, indulge in curious speculations about things like who or what is 666. A quick survey of all those who have been identified will tell us that no one knows who he or she was or will be. I believe there is a much better way of looking at that passage that we will come to later. So much for what I will not do.

What I will do is try to bring out the main message of Revelation so that you will no longer have to approach the book as though it cannot be understood. Furthermore, you will be able to discern truth from error when people misquote Revelation. I will also delineate clearly the main thrust of each passage sufficiently for you to lead a Bible study on it if you wish. There are some Bible study questions at the conclusion of each chapter.

The Purpose

Verses 1 to 3 are the introduction to the whole book and give us right from the start the twin purposes of this revelation, the first of which is simply the revelation of Jesus Christ. It is Christ revealing Himself to us. The word *revelation* in the Greek means "manifestation, appearing, or unveiling." It is not the unveiling of Satan, or the revelation of 666. It is to reveal more of Christ, His Kingdom, and His majesty. As A.W. Tozer says, "The Revelation is a great book because it is the revelation of Jesus Christ." It is not for the purpose of satisfying our curiosity.

The second purpose is to show us, in broad terms, what must take place in the future. It says in verse 1 that God gave us the book *"to show his servants what must soon take place."* Once again, the reason for this is not so that our thirst for the unknown may be quenched, but that we might know how to respond as His people in those times. As Eugene Peterson wrote: "The intent of Revelation is not to inform us about God but to involve us in God." It is not to give us a whole lot of facts, but to tell us how to live. Therefore, the book was written to reveal and not to hide, to disclose and not to conceal. In other words, it is designed in such a way that we as common people are able to understand it. It was written, not for the academic theologian, but for the ordinary person.

At this point, let me share with you three pointers that will help us understand the book. First, the chapters and verses are not necessarily chronological. For instance, events described in chapter 15 do not necessarily occur after those of chapter 14. Or, just because chapter 12 follows chapter 11 does not mean that the events described happen in this order. It means that we should not try to map out history according to the order of the chapters.

Second, not all symbolic descriptions are to be taken literally. Revelation contains a large amount of symbolic language because it is apocalyptic literature, describing great, dramatic and extraordinary events of the future. This is not to say that everything in the book is symbolic and nothing can be taken at face value, but it does mean we would be unwise to take certain descriptions literally when they have symbolic meaning. For instance, the star called Wormwood that falls from the sky and poisons our rivers, in Revelation 8:11, is not necessarily a comet hitting the earth. A literal approach would take that interpretation, but I believe unnecessarily, since *Wormwood* is a word found in the Old Testament that means "bitterness" and that applies logically to the context of chapter 8.

Third, Revelation is a picture book. In a sense, it is more like a movie than a book and is better seen than read. We are to see it with our imaginations, feel it with our senses and be impacted by it in our emotions. It is not just for the analysis of the mind, but for the quickening of the hearts. We are to feel the impact of it in its totality, like a blockbuster movie, and not be stuck in analyzing a particular frame. Imagine watching "Star Wars" and stopping the screening to ask why there is a scratch on Darth Vader's helmet when he is fighting Luke Skywalker in the final scene. That is exactly what we will have done if we excessively analyze a particular verse in a chapter without experiencing the impact of that chapter. We will have missed the forest for the trees.

Now to some brief comments on verses 1 to 4. It is worth noting, in verse 1, that this revelation is given specifically to the servants of Christ. The Greek word is that for a bondslave (*doulos*). It is not the word *diakonos*, which is the word for deacon and is usually translated as "servant." If we want to hear from God, we must first ask ourselves if we are slaves of Christ. *Doulos* emphasizes the importance of submission and total obedience to our Master. Some wonder why they don't hear from God when their hearts are far from obedient. Are we ready to obey? Do we submit to His will? It is not just those who hear that are blessed, but those who hear and heed this word of prophecy.

The Reason for Revelation

In verse 4, John blesses his hearers with grace and peace, but note that grace comes before peace. The order is important, as there can be no peace without grace. Genuine peace is that which the world cannot give and which can only be experienced after the reception of grace. Peace with God is for those who have a relationship with Jesus Christ through grace. The serenity of God reigns in those who are immersed in His grace.

The First Witness

Verses 5 to 8 give us a beautiful description of who Christ is and what He has done for us. We see that He is the faithful witness, the firstborn from the dead and the ruler of the kings of the earth. What an encouragement this would have been to the Christians being persecuted and who would eventually be martyred for their faith. The Greek word for "witness" is also the word for "martyr," and Jesus is described as the faithful martyr. Those who would die for their faith in the first century A.D. were reminded that Jesus the martyr had gone before them. He is also the firstborn from the dead, and just as they follow Christ unto death, they will rise again as He rose. Furthermore, as Christ is the ruler of all, they will not only rise with Him but also reign with Him.

John tells his hearers that this is the same Jesus who loves them, who has freed them from sin and who has given them heavenly citizenship. This was no comfort to those who loved Roman citizenship more than their heavenly inheritance, but to those who were persecuted by the state this was no small assurance. They belong to a Kingdom greater than Rome, and so do we. In view of the resurgence of nationalistic and ethnic sentiments across the world, it is worth reminding ourselves that Christians are first and foremost citizens of the Kingdom of God. Our race, culture and country will have to come second to our heavenly calling.

The passage ends by reminding the hearers that this same Jesus is coming back for His beloved (Revelation 1:7). *"Look, he is coming with the clouds, and every eye will see him, even those who pierced him; and all the peoples of the earth will mourn because of him. So shall it be! Amen."* That Day of the Lord will be an extremely happy day, but it will also be a sad one. To all those who look forward to His coming it will be a day of unbeatable joy, but to those who have rejected His salvation and have stubbornly kept Him at arm's length it will be a day of inexpressible sadness. Many will mourn because of Him.

" *'I am the Alpha and the Omega,' says the Lord God, 'who is, and who was, and who is to come, the Almighty'* " (verse 8). Some of John's first-century hearers were facing persecution; others were being warned of impending hardship. The encouragement Jesus gave to them through John was to take a short look at their problems but a long look at Him. We will do well to follow that exhortation in the face of discouragement. He is, after all, the Beginning and the End — and everything in between.

Questions for Private Study and Discussion

1. Why do you think some Christians avoid the book of Revelation? How do you feel about the book?

2. In what way is it unhealthy to indulge in excessive speculations about the book? What is the purpose of the Revelation?

3. What does it mean to take a short look at your problem and a long look at God?

4. How would verses 5 to 8 have encouraged the original recipients of John's letter? How does your situation compare with theirs?

5. In what way would the Second Coming of Christ be both a happy and a sad day?

6. How can the study of Revelation help prepare you for the Second Coming?

7. What is it about this chapter that impressed you most?

Chapter 2

PORTRAIT OF THE LIVING CHRIST

Revelation 1:9-20:

I, John, your brother and companion in the suffering and kingdom and patient endurance that are ours in Jesus, was on the island of Patmos because of the word of God and the testimony of Jesus. {10} On the Lord's Day I was in the Spirit, and I heard behind me a loud voice like a trumpet, {11} which said: "Write on a scroll what you see and send it to the seven churches: to Ephesus, Smyrna, Pergamum, Thyatira, Sardis, Philadelphia and Laodicea."

{12} I turned around to see the voice that was speaking to me. And when I turned I saw seven golden lampstands, {13} and among the lampstands was someone "like a son of man," dressed in a robe reaching down to his feet and with a golden sash around his chest. {14} His head and hair were white like wool, as white as snow, and his eyes were like blazing fire. {15} His feet were like bronze glowing in a furnace, and his voice was like the sound of rushing waters. {16} In his right hand he held seven stars, and out of his mouth came a sharp double-edged sword. His face was like the sun shining in all its brilliance.

{17} When I saw him, I fell at his feet as though dead. Then he placed his right hand on me and said: "Do not be afraid. I am the First and the Last. {18} I am the Living One; I was dead, and behold I am alive for ever and ever! And I hold the keys of death and Hades.

{19} "Write, therefore, what you have seen, what is now and what will take place later. {20} The mystery of the seven stars that you saw in my right hand and of the seven golden lampstands is this: The seven stars are the angels of the seven churches, and the seven lampstands are the seven churches."

How on earth does one write on a passage such as this without letting words get in the way? Can words describe a rainbow for us better than actually seeing one? Like describing a glorious sunset across the ocean, it is far better to behold the sight than to imagine the words. The apostle John, unfortunately, did not have a video camera with him when the vision of Christ's portrait was revealed to him. He could only write down what he saw in words that he thought best represented the picture. We need to be careful, therefore, when approaching this portrait of Christ (verses 13-16) not to let words get in the way in our analysis. We must not tear the rainbow apart, so to speak, in our examination of the vision. We need to behold its beauty and let that speak for itself. In this regard, we need more than ever the aid of the Spirit of revelation and illumination to see what He wants to reveal. Like all spiritual truths, we need to perceive it in our hearts as well as understand it with our minds.

The passage under consideration is very important for two reasons. First, it gives us a powerful picture of who Jesus is. If someone was to ask us: "what is your image of Jesus?" what would our answer be? How we see Jesus affects the way we think of Him and relate to Him. For example, if our image of Jesus is only that of a man hanging on the cross, we are likely to remember His suffering and pain on our behalf. On this note, the book of Revelation does portray Jesus as the Lamb that was slain, and does it often. But in verses 13 to 16 of chapter 1 He is portrayed not as the suffering Jesus, but as the awesome, ascended, post-resurrection Christ — risen in power and full of glory! He is no longer hanging on the cross, but has risen indeed with victory over death and Hades. In the previous chapter we are exhorted to take a long look at Jesus. Now it is worth asking ourselves, "When we take a long look at Christ, what do we see?" William MacArthur states that this vision is "the only authentic portrait of our Savior and Lord." Whether or not we agree that it is the "only" authentic portrait, it is the portrait of verses 13 to 16, and a great one at that.

The second reason for the significance of this portrait is that this is the One who is authoring the letters to the seven churches that follow in chapters 2 and 3. It will help us further appreciate the seven letters if we see clearly this portrait of the One who is writing it. The messages in those letters will become more powerful when we behold clearly this portrait of its author.

John's Introduction

We know from verse 9 that John was in exile on Patmos. Patmos is a small island around 30 miles wide and was used for the settlement of offenders. John was no criminal, but he was persecuted. How did John look upon his own circumstances as a ninety-year-old man in exile? What was his perspective on his suffering?

We can learn much in verse 9 concerning John's perspective on the Christian life. In verse 9 it says, *"I, John, your brother and companion in the suffering and kingdom and patient endurance that are ours in Jesus ... ."* John sees himself as a privileged partner with other Christians in three things: suffering, the Kingdom of God and patient endurance.

The word *suffering* in the original language relates to persecution, tribulation, troubles and trials. John saw himself as a fellow partner in suffering for the sake of the Gospel. For John, suffering is part and parcel of what it means to be in the Kingdom of God. It is an interesting paradox that the Kingdom of God refers to the reign and rule of God. Where God rules, there His Kingdom is. Yet, while they share in the powerful reign of God, suffering is coexistent. This is a seeming paradox, because how can suffering and the reign of God be mutually coexistent? The reason for this is what some, like Gordon Fee, have termed the "already-not-yet" nature of God's Kingdom. God's Kingdom came in Jesus while He was on earth; it is still coming with every sinner who repents; but it will come fully only when Christ returns. We live in the "in-between" period where there is the tension of the Kingdom having come but not fully. That is why Christians share both in suffering through persecution and in God's Kingdom at the same time. In view of this, "patient endurance" is also ours in Jesus, says John to his fellow believers.

It is difficult for Christians living in industrialized countries such as those in the West to accept that suffering and patient endurance are integral to the Kingdom of God. In some branches of Christianity, suffering is a taboo topic that is poorly handled. However, while we do not look for suffering, it is an inevitable part of our human experience. Even if we are not persecuted for the faith, suffering is a reality that exists in many forms. A mother losing an unborn child, a husband losing his wife through cancer, being long-term unemployed — these are but a few examples of this reality. Not only do we need to learn to cope with suffering, but our perspective of what it means to be in the Kingdom and that of patient endurance should in itself bear witness to our risen Lord. If suffering is part of the human condition, let us suffer well. Of course, there are also times when God heals powerfully and miraculously, and we must never forget that.

In verse 10 we read that John was in the Spirit when he received the vision. Interestingly, it was also on the Lord's Day: *"On the Lord's Day I was in the Spirit."* It is encouraging to note that John was deep in worship on "Sunday." What does it mean to be "in the Spirit"? Robert Mounce contends that John was in an ecstatic trance. The Amplified version of the Bible says that John was *"rapt in His power."* Ephesians 6 puts "in the Spirit" in the context of prayer and worship. It is not hard to imagine that John was caught up in the Spirit as he was deep in prayer and worship on the Lord's Day!

What would have happened if John had not been in the Spirit? He might not have received the vision of Revelation! A fascinating thought indeed — with great consequences! When we are in trouble or hardship, do we enter into the Spirit? If God has a message for us, perhaps a crucial word of instruction or comfort, how can He deliver it to us except through His Spirit? And if we are not "in the Spirit"?

Vision of the Risen Christ

John turned to see who it was that was speaking to Him. He saw an incredible, indescribable vision of the risen Christ. In being careful not to "unweave the rainbow," each aspect of this vision will be examined on its own only briefly. The parts will then be put together to give us a wonderful portrait of Jesus. We will see that the whole is greater than the sum of its parts.

First, John saw one "like a son of man." What does "son of man" refer to? Daniel 7:13 gives an important clue: *"In my vision at night I looked, and there before me was one like a son of man, coming with the clouds of heaven."*

The term was used by Daniel to depict the Messiah. This is also the first occasion where "son of man" referred to the Messiah. When Jesus was on earth, the title He most commonly used for Himself was "Son of Man." In the context of Daniel, Jesus was referring to Himself as the Messiah. Without a doubt, we Christians know that indeed Jesus was and is the Messiah as prophesied in Scripture. Worthy of note too is that *son* in Hebrew means "of the order of." Thus, *"son of God"* means "of the order of God," and *"son of man"* means "of the order of man." In other words, *"son of man"* also means "man" or "human being." The Good News Bible translates the phrase in Revelation 1:13 as *"looked like a human being."* Therefore, the humanity of Christ the Messiah is emphasized here.

Second, He was dressed in a robe reaching down to His feet and with a golden sash around His chest. This is the high priestly garment as depicted in Exodus 28:4 and 39:29. The high priestly role of Jesus is emphasized here. The book of Hebrews makes the priestly ministry role of Jesus abundantly clear: *"Therefore, since we have a great high priest who has gone through the heavens, Jesus the Son of God, let us hold firmly to the faith we profess. For we do not have a high priest who is unable to sympathize with our weaknesses, but we have one who has been tempted in every way, just as we are — yet was without sin"* (Hebrews 4:14-15). One major difference between Jesus' garment and the high priestly garment of Exodus is the sash. Jesus' is a golden sash, highlighting His royalty. He is our royal high priest. Thus what we see here is the royal high priestly ministry of Jesus, representing us before the throne and interceding on our behalf. What a friend we have in Jesus!

Third, His head and hair were white like wool. Interestingly, the Father was described in such terms in Daniel 7:9: *"As I looked, thrones were set in place, and the Ancient of Days took his seat. His clothing was as white as snow; the hair of his head was white like wool."* What does white symbolize in the Bible? It can refer to one who is dead or leprous, which does not apply here. It can also refer to purity, holiness and righteousness: " *'Come now, let us reason together,' says the* Lord. *'Though your sins are like scarlet, they shall be as white as snow; though they are red as crimson, they shall be like wool'* " (Isaiah 1:18). On seventeen occasions in Revelation the word refers to the saints — righteous, holy and pure. In the New Testament, white can also symbolize glory, as in the transfiguration of Jesus. Therefore, in this description we see the glory and holiness of Jesus.

Fourth, His "eyes were like blazing fire." Eyes refer to sight and vision. This is the One who has a penetrating gaze and perfect vision. As He walks among the seven churches, He sees their true state of affairs. Like someone possessing X-ray vision, He is able to see into our hearts with accuracy.

Fifth, His feet were like bronze glowing in a furnace. This is in contrast to the statue in the dream that Daniel interpreted that had feet of clay — unstable and weak. Christ comes with feet of authority and permanence, crushing all enemies under Him. Burnished, or glowing, bronze also refers to one who has been refined through the fire of suffering, matching the image of the Lamb that was slain. Christ derived His authority and victory through suffering. This aspect of Christ reminds us of His authority and the permanence of His Kingdom.

Sixth, His voice was like the sound of rushing waters. Ezekiel 43:2 says, *"And I saw the glory of the God of Israel coming from the east. His voice was like the roar of rushing waters, and the land was radiant with his glory."* The voice of the risen Christ is loud, commanding and thunderous, like the sound of a huge waterfall.

Seventh, out of his mouth came a sharp double-edged sword. Revelation 2:16 helps us to understand this description: *"I will soon come to you and will fight against them with the sword of my mouth."* Warfare is alluded to here. In Revelation 19, the sharp sword out of His mouth refers to divine judgment. *"Out of his mouth comes a sharp sword with which to strike down the nations. 'He will rule them with an iron scepter.' He treads the winepress of the fury of the wrath of God Almighty"* (Revelation 19:15). All of this description speaks of divine wrath and judgment.

Eighth, His face was like the sun shining in all its brilliance. Have you ever tried looking into the midday sun? It is definitely not an advisable thing to do. The face of Christ is brilliant like the midday sun. The Greek word translated *brilliance* here is *dunamis*, the word for "power."

What an incredible portrait of our Lord and Savior Jesus Christ! His humanity and divinity are both portrayed. Christ is fully man and fully God — crucified in weakness but raised in power. His head and hair shines with glory and holiness. His face beams with splendor and radiates with power. His eyes are fiery and penetrating. His mouth speaks the word of judgment. His feet come with crushing authority, permanently establishing His eternal Kingdom. His voice thunders like a waterfall.

John's Response

It is no wonder that when John saw the risen Christ, he *"fell at his feet as though dead."* What else could one do under such an immense display of power and glory emanating from the Second Person of the Godhead? This was not the Christ John remembered on earth. John had never seen his Savior in this manner.

John had no questions left for his Savior. He could have had many questions in his mind before this display of awesomeness. It would have been natural and understandable. John was in exile, away from his flock and his fellow workers. All the other apostles were dead. Peter had been crucified upside down and Paul beheaded. Ninety-year-old John was the only apostle left, and he was now in exile. His churches were being persecuted, and some fellow workers had been martyred. Satan seemed to be winning. It would have been excusable for John to feel a little depressed. He might have thought, *What happened? What went wrong? Is God still with us? Why, Lord?* But he had no questions to ask when facing his Savior. He could only respond by falling at His feet as though dead.

I have heard many Christians say that when they meet God in Heaven, they will have a host of questions to ask Him. I think, perhaps not. When we see God face-to-face, we will be so awestruck that we will most likely respond exactly as John did. We will fall facedown in worship, and weep with tears of inexpressible emotion.

Notice how Jesus responded in verse 17: *"Then he placed his right hand on me and said: 'Do not be afraid.'"* It sounds much like "Fear not, little flock," a phrase often repeated by Christ while on earth. Indeed, it is the same Jesus! John might have thought to himself, *Is that really You, Lord?* The high priestly ministry of Jesus was immediately evident: His touch of gentleness, His compassion. The mighty and awesome glorified Christ did not command: "Stand up, you wimp!" but placed His hand on John and said, "Do not be afraid." Could He be saying the same thing to you today?

This is the One walking among the seven golden lampstands — the seven churches of Asia Minor. This is He who holds the seven stars in His hand — the leadership of the churches, (both physical and spiritual). The keys of death and Hades are in His hands. He has overcome. Victory is assured for those who trust in Him.

Conclusion

In conclusion, what can we see in this passage?

- We see the importance of the Church. Jesus walks among His churches, holding their leadership in His Hands.

- We see the smallness of humanity compared with the eternity and awesomeness of the resurrected Christ.

- We see the greatness of human worth, that such a One should die for us.

- We see the insignificance of earthly kingdoms and worldly affairs compared with the permanence of God and of the Kingdom of Christ.

- We see the glory and majesty of our Savior Jesus who holds the keys of death in His hands.

Questions for Private Study and Discussion

1. How is it that "suffering" is so much a part of God's Kingdom?

2. How does John's portrait of the risen Christ impress you?

3. In what ways was John's response in verse 17 appropriate?

4. What would you like to ask Jesus when you see Him face-to-face?

5. Name five lessons you can learn from this passage. How might they affect you this week?

Chapter 3

LOVE: THE MESSAGE TO
THE CHURCH IN EPHESUS

Revelation 2:1-7:

"To the angel of the church in Ephesus write:
These are the words of him who holds the seven stars in his right
hand and walks among the seven golden lampstands: {2} I know
your deeds, your hard work and your perseverance. I know that you
cannot tolerate wicked men, that you have tested those who claim
to be apostles but are not, and have found them false. {3} You have
persevered and have endured hardships for my name, and have not
grown weary.
{4} Yet I hold this against you: You have forsaken your first love. {5}
Remember the height from which you have fallen! Repent and do the
things you did at first. If you do not repent, I will come to you and
remove your lampstand from its place. {6} But you have this in your
favor: You hate the practices of the Nicolaitans, which I also hate.
{7} He who has an ear, let him hear what the Spirit says to the
churches. To him who overcomes, I will give the right to eat from
the tree of life, which is in the paradise of God."

Before we delve into this letter to the church at Ephesus, I would like
to make four comments about these seven letters as a whole. First, the
aim of these letters is not to condemn but to set free. It is the experience
of some, when they read these seven letters or hear sermons on them,
to feel the burden of guilt. The reason might be that the words of Jesus
expressed here are sharper than a double-edged sword. They are pierc-
ing, revealing and uncompromising. So it is worth reminding ourselves
from the beginning that these seven letters were given by Jesus to set

them, and us, free from anything that might hinder them or us from being effective Christians. It does so by convicting us of sin. It is not the aim of the Spirit to trap us under guilt — that is what the evil one does. When Christ points His finger at our sin, we need to quickly and genuinely repent in order to move on.

Second, the lessons of these seven letters will apply to most Christians in different spiritual seasons. In other words, depending on our circumstances, what may not speak to us now might well be relevant in a month or a year's time. Therefore, we need to heed these lessons repeatedly in our lives. None of us are immune from the spiritual dangers or diseases faced by these churches. For instance, we may not have left our "first love" now, but it does not mean that will never happen to us in the future. If and when it does, we need to heed the message to the church at Ephesus.

Third, as one might deduce from the above, I am not convinced that these seven letters depict seven distinct periods of church history. It has been argued, for instance, that Christendom is now into the final "Laodicean" stage where the church is lukewarm. This is the suggestion of some, but their arguments are far from persuasive. In fact, Revelation 2:7 lends evidence to the universal application of these seven letters regardless of the period of history we may be in: *"He who has an ear, let him hear what the Spirit says to the churches."* Each of the seven churches was to hear and heed the lessons of the other churches. The seven "letters" are in actuality part and parcel of the entire book of Revelation. The book is one huge letter sent to all churches to be heeded at all times.

Finally, for each of the seven letters to the seven churches I will give a key word that attempts to summarize each letter. It will represent either a quality we should emulate or a warning we should heed. The key word for the church at Ephesus is "love."

Christ Among His Churches

Revelation 2:1 reminds us who is giving this message to the Ephesian Christians: *"To the angel of the church in Ephesus write: These are the words of him who holds the seven stars in his right hand and walks among the seven golden lampstands."* It is the ascended-resurrected Christ of chapter 1. He holds the leadership, both human and angelic beings, of the Church in

His hands. He protects and directs His Church. It is His Church, bought by His blood.

Christ is walking among His churches. He is also walking in the midst of the church at Ephesus. *Why is that?* one may wonder. *Why is He walking among His people?* It is to discern the state, the true condition, of His people. With eyes of blazing fire He sees our true condition as Christians. He knows our hearts — our struggles, victories and defeats. He gives an accurate assessment of our true situation. Like a skilled doctor, He diagnoses and offers an effective treatment.

What is the condition of your heart at present? As you read this, take comfort from the doctor's diagnosis. He will speak the truth, and He is compassionate. He is the one who placed His hand on John and said, "Do not be afraid."

Christ's Commendations

In verses 2 and 3, Christ gives seven commendations before the rebuke. Note the ratio of seven positive remarks to one constructive criticism. It is unfortunate that some preachers have called the Ephesian church a "loveless church." This is not helpful, as it focuses on the negative attribute at the expense of the positive ones. As we shall see, the church was in actuality a strong church with many good qualities. Christ's rebuke was given in the context of many commendations, which highlights both the power of His diagnosis and the potency of this lesson for us.

Here also is a lesson in offering constructive criticism. Christ, the awesome Risen One, did not begin by "shooting from the hip," but with affirmative words. We can learn from this. When we offer words of rebuke to others, let us begin with affirmation. All of us have strengths and weaknesses. Beginning with affirmation helps us not to be overly critical of others. It prevents us from narrowly focusing on the weaknesses of others at the expense of their strengths. As in a sandwich, when giving criticisms to others, we need to place the meat of a rebuke between the bread of affirmation.

Hard work:

One of the commendations Christ gave was for their *"hard work."* In the original Greek, the meaning of this phrase was "labor to the point of weariness." What might this *"hard work"* have referred to for the congregation at Ephesus? The situation they were facing might give us a clue here. Ephesus was a city filled with weird religious teachings, and the potential for false doctrines in the church was abundant. In Ephesus was the great temple of Diana, standing sixty feet tall and supported by 127 marble pillars. It was one of the seven wonders of the ancient world. In Acts, we see that the practice of sorcery and magic was rampant in Ephesus. Paul warned the elders of the church of false teachers, wolves, in Acts 20:29. Can you imagine the amount of work that would have gone into countering these false teachers and their false doctrines? Christ commended this church for going through the laborious task of testing false teachers and false apostles. Putting it in our context, this would not have been a church that tolerates pastors who do not believe in the resurrection or that condones the practice of homosexuality. The congregation at Ephesus had consistently fought off any who would water down the Gospel of Jesus Christ.

It is no small task to ward off false doctrines and heretical teachings in a church. Numerous "Bible studies" would need to be held, to say the least. Many will hold differing opinions within the same congregation. Consider the range of issues that face the twenty-first-century Church: the role of women, liberation theology, the baptism of the Holy Spirit, speaking in tongues and healing, end-time Israel, prosperity theology, homosexuality, divorce and remarriage and many more. As the Church enters the Postmodern Era, there is much to learn from this quality of the Ephesian church.

Endured hardships:

Not only did the church at Ephesus have internal troubles arising from false teaching, it experienced external persecution from the emperor Domitian. Emperor Domitian demanded to be addressed as "lord and god." The consequence for not bowing to emperor worship was manifold. First, there was shame in not being nationalistic, or loyal to Rome. Second, economic difficulties arose from not being allowed to join trade guilds. Third, some faced imprisonment and martyrdom.

This reminded me of an elderly Chinese pastor whom I met in Shanghai the first time I visited China. He had been in jail for more than twenty years for the faith. He did not renounce Christianity but maintained faithfulness to the Gospel. It was a moving experience to hear his story. Accounts of persecution from the communists are often hair-raising.

Not grown weary:

Not only did the Ephesian church face both internal and external pressure, Christ commended them for not growing weary! The church was not young or new. By the time John wrote his letter, it was forty years old as a church. No wonder Christ commended their perseverance. As can be seen, the church was great in many ways. She had qualities of endurance and faithfulness in the face of suffering great tribulation.

I wonder how we might have fared in the same circumstance. How do we handle external pressure, perhaps from nonbelieving colleagues or friends? How do we deal with the stressors that attack us from without? And what about pressures from within our own family or church? At the end of a long period of trial, are we weary of it all? I do not think Christ is referring here to the feeling of weariness in terms of emotion. The Ephesian church might have felt weary, but they persevered in their actions. Therefore, their perseverance is proven by their deeds, not their emotions. There is so much going for the Christians at Ephesus!

Christ's Rebukes

The sad thing about this church is that not only did Christ want a bride who was faithful, He wanted a bride who was madly in love with Him. The Good News Bible puts verse 4 this way: *"You do not love me now as you did at first."* This church probably left her love at two levels: vertical and horizontal. She left her first love for God and her affection for one another. When we are no longer in love with Jesus, it becomes difficult to love others.

The Ephesians needed to fall in love again with their Savior. There is a very important lesson here for all Christians: Christianity is more than holding to the right teaching; it is primarily a love relationship with the Living Christ. The Christian faith is more than a set of doctrines, however orthodox; it is being a child of God and the bride of Christ.

Risen Lamb, Empowered Saints

The church in Ephesus was faithful in her service to Christ, but although service to God is important, even more so was her relationship with Him. Service ought to be an overflow of our love for Him. Steve Green has a beautiful song called "The Mission," which expresses this truth profoundly. It says: "To love the Lord our God is the heartbeat of our mission, the spring from which our service overflows." God's love in our hearts is the fountain from which effective ministry flows.

I remembered having this lesson brought home to me in a significant way some years ago at the first church I pastored. I was going through a period where worries about ministry were plaguing me. Yes, I prayed much about it, but all my prayers were only intercessory prayers. There was little worship and spending time in His presence. Furthermore, my intercessions were out of worry and not faith. This went on for some time until I was as dry as a desert. I knew I needed a breakthrough of refreshing. One morning the renewal came in a most unexpected way. I was pacing the house when I felt the Spirit say to me, "Sit down." I obeyed and sat on a chair. Then the Spirit impressed this upon me strongly in my heart: "I love you." I thought to myself, *Yes, I know that in my mind.* But hearing the Spirit's reaffirmation was refreshing. The Spirit continued, and this was what blew me away: "I love you so much that I will not let anything get in the way of your relationship with Me. And if you let anything get in the way of our love relationship, I will destroy that thing — even if it's your ministry." It was a powerful experience. God loves me so much that He will let nothing get in the way — not even service for His Kingdom. Nowadays I attempt to remind myself of that often, even as I serve in the ministry of Living Impact.

In Ephesians chapter 3, Paul urges us to be rooted and established in God's love, to grasp how wide and high, long and deep His love is for us (see verses 16-19). Ten years ago, when my wife and I first moved into the house we are now living in, someone gave us a gum (eucalyptus) tree seedling in a six-inch pot. We carefully planted it in our front garden, digging a hole and filling it with good soil. Now it is the tallest tree in the garden, more than fifteen feet high. That little gum tree would never have grown to its full potential if it had remained in the six-inch pot. It needed good soil in order to develop according to its genetic code.

Similarly, we as God's children need to be rooted in the soil of His love if we are to grow to our full potential as Christians.

The church at Ephesus in Revelation 2 was failing to be a bride in love. She was faithful, but Christ wanted love. What a price to pay for good works, orthodoxy, correct teaching and soundness of doctrine. Was it worth it? No, not at the expense of what is the core ingredient of Christianity — a love relationship. Christ gave them no excuse. He did not say, "I'll let you off the hook this time," or "It's okay because you are faithful." In verses 4 and 5, He said, *"Yet I hold this against you: You have forsaken your first love. Remember the height from which you have fallen! Repent and do the things you did at first. If you do not repent, I will come to you and remove your lampstand from its place."*

The church was commanded to repent and do the things they did at first. They were initially zealous for the presence of God. Similarly, we need to spend time in His presence — to fellowship with Him. Worship is also essential to renewal. They also shared the Good News of love with others in Ephesus. The Great Commission was what they did. Therefore, these were two things they were admonished to do again: enjoy the fellowship of His presence, and discharge the Great Commission.

It was out of love that Christ rebuked them. His love compelled Him to rebuke them. At stake was the core essential of the Christian faith — loving God. The first commandment is to love the Lord our God with all our heart, mind, soul and strength. Take this away and we will be left with pharisaical legalism. Christ could not let that happen to the Christians at Ephesus. He loved them too much. It is worth asking ourselves, "When Christ comes again, will He find us in love with Him? Or have we set our hearts on something else?"

Questions for Private Study and Discussion

1. Why is it that we should feel neither guilty nor proud when reading these seven letters to the seven churches?

2. What is the practical significance of Christ walking among His churches?

3. Why is it a mistake to label the Ephesus church as "loveless"?

4. What can we learn from the strengths of this church at Ephesus?

5. What did Jesus have against them, and why was it important?

6. How can we prevent ourselves from falling into the same error as the Ephesians did?

Chapter 4

FAITHFULNESS: THE MESSAGE TO THE CHURCH IN SMYRNA

Revelation 2:8-11:

> "To the angel of the church in Smyrna write:
> These are the words of him who is the First and the Last, who died and came to life again. {9} I know your afflictions and your poverty—yet you are rich! I know the slander of those who say they are Jews and are not, but are a synagogue of Satan. {10} Do not be afraid of what you are about to suffer. I tell you, the devil will put some of you in prison to test you, and you will suffer persecution for ten days. Be faithful, even to the point of death, and I will give you the crown of life.
> {11} He who has an ear, let him hear what the Spirit says to the churches. He who overcomes will not be hurt at all by the second death."

The key word for this letter is "faithfulness," even in the midst of adversity, suffering and martyrdom. The challenge for us is to be faithful in following Jesus regardless of circumstances, and faithful to our callings in spite of the cost. The Smyrnan Christians were living out the exhortation (rebuke) Christ gave the church at Ephesus. The Ephesian Christians have abandoned their first love, but the Smyrnan believers abandoned themselves to the love of God. The result was a "perfect" church, if ever there was one.

The city of Smyrna is the only one of the seven cities of Asia Minor that is still in existence. It is the modern-day city of Izmir. Have you ever wondered what Smyrna was like in the days of John? Was it like a small country town that almost no one has ever heard of, such as Dimboola?

Or perhaps it was a larger and more popular place in the country, such as Ballarat, a well known gold mining town in Australia. In fact, it was probably more like Sydney or San Francisco, a thriving city of international recognition. For someone in those days to be living in Smyrna is like us living in a big, booming, advanced metropolis.

There are some interesting similarities between Sydney and Smyrna that are worth noting. For instance, both have a harbor. Sydney is known for the Opera House; Smyrna for her "crown," a circle of beautiful public buildings which ringed the summit of Mount Pagos like a diadem. Sydney has some popular academic courses and graduate schools, such as the Master of Business Administration course at the Graduate School of Management; Smyrna was famous for her science and medicine. Sydney competed successfully to host the Olympics; Smyrna was a rival bidder to Ephesus to hold the famous Games of Asia Minor. Smyrna was also rich in trade and had a booming population of two hundred thousand.

Poor Yet Rich

It is to this group of Christians living in this wealthy city of Smyrna that Jesus wrote: *"I know your afflictions and your poverty — yet you are rich"* (verse 9). One commentator explained the Smyrnans' afflictions as a "burden that crushes." Have you ever experienced a "burden that crushes"? Perhaps it was a physical ailment such as cancer, or a heavy financial debt. The Smyrnans were poor, and the Greek word for *poverty* equates to *beggary*. It is the same word used in 2 Corinthians 8:2: *"Out of the most severe trial, their overflowing joy and their extreme POVERTY welled up in rich generosity."* There is not much pride in being poor in a rich, thriving city. Think of the possible insults thrown at them by unbelievers: "Why are you not blessed? Do you not claim to be a child of God? Why then are you living like a beggar?" There would be little room in the church of Smyrna for our modern-day "prosperity Gospel."

The irony is that Jesus thought of them as rich — spiritually. It reminds us of the parable of the rich fool. He was rich in the world but poor toward God. It is not that his riches were a sin in itself. After all, Old Testament heroes like Abraham, King David and Solomon possessed great wealth. The problem was that he was poor spiritually, and his riches prevented his condition from being remedied. In contrast, the Smyrnans were beggarly in terms of wealth, but rich in Christ and in spirituality.

Persecution

Some of us may wonder why they were so poor when the city of Smyrna was financially booming. After all, the economy was good. The reason is persecution. It was not because they were stupid or lazy. They were persecuted by two parties, the Romans and the Jews.

There were two main charges the Romans laid against them. First, they were accused of being atheists, an interesting charge indeed for Christians who claim to believe in God! The problem was that these Christians had no idols and no shrines, and they only talked about Jesus. Second, they were accused of disloyalty. Loyalty to Rome was very important to the city of Smyrna. Historically, she was an ally of Rome before Rome was even acknowledged in the region. This loyalty was also related to Roman emperor worship — a sign of nationalism. In A.D. 26 the city shrewdly petitioned Emperor Tiberius to allow them to build a temple to his deity.

The second part of verse 9 says, *"I know the slander of those who say they are Jews and are not, but are a synagogue of Satan."* There were three slanders made toward them by the Jews. First, they indulged in cannibalism. This was a misinterpretation of Holy Communion — eating the body of Jesus and drinking His blood. Second, they were accused of lust and immorality. The Communion was known as the "agape" (love) feast, and there was an element of privacy and "secrecy" in the act — one had to be a Christian. Third, they were accused of breaking up homes — when pagans converted, some might have been excommunicated from their families. But Jesus called the Smyrnan Jews a synagogue of Satan, a great irony since pharisaical Jews claimed to be God's people. The true people of God in the eyes of Jesus are those who have received Him as Savior and Lord.

It is probable that not many unbelievers had flocked to this church. It was probably small in size. The consequences of becoming a Christian were there for all to see. The Smyrnan Christians were persecuted by both Jews and non-Jews. They were poor and despised as a result of their faith. The consequences were real, and severe.

How did Jesus respond to their suffering? Did He promise to remove it? The answer is in verse 10: *"Do not be afraid of what you are about to suffer. I tell you, the devil will put some of you in prison to test you, and you will suffer persecution for ten days."* No, Christ did not promise to eliminate their tribulation. Worth noting, though, is that tribulation comes from the devil. God allowed it for the purpose of testing them. They were exhorted not be afraid. Instead, they were to fear God and not man. Revelation 15:4 says: *"Who will not fear you, O Lord, and bring glory to your name? For you alone are holy. All nations will come and worship before you, for your righteous acts have been revealed."* Consider Hebrews 13:6: *"So we say with confidence, 'The Lord is my helper; I will not be afraid. What can man do to me?' "* Their persecution will be for ten days, not to be taken literally, since "ten" is one of those biblical numbers. It means that their persecution will be short, for a specified period, and complete. It must run its course.

Be Faithful

Revelation 2:10 reads, *"Be faithful, even to the point of death, and I will give you the crown of life."* This is a strange paradox: in dying faithful they receive life. This was the challenge Christ gave to them: Be faithful, even if it means martyrdom. Jesus was saying to them: "I've been there — I died and rose again" (see verse 8). Remember that in Revelation 1:5, Jesus called Himself *"the faithful witness."*

Some from this church at Smyrna were in fact martyred, as recorded in Church history. The most famous was Polycarp. He was the bishop of Smyrna appointed by the apostle John. He was the twelfth martyr of the Christian Church. Polycarp was burned alive at 86 years of age because he refused to acknowledge Caesar as lord. The Jews conspired against him and even collected the wood for his burning, one Sabbath day! Before his death, Polycarp uttered these words, *"Eighty and six years I have served Him, and He hath done me no wrong; how then can I blaspheme my King who saved me?"*

There is a cost to discipleship. There is a cost in obeying His call. The command that went out to the Smyrnans was to be faithful — at all costs. There is always a cost involved for those who want to be faithful to their God and to their calling. What has been your cost in obeying His call? If it is your true calling, it is worth the sacrifice.

For me, resigning from a well-paid pastoral ministry to begin Living Impact, a mission reaching the "10/40 Window," had a real cost. Financially, I received no salary. My wife agreed to return to the work force to support the family, which she did willingly and joyfully (PTL!). For Ling, it was and is a real sacrifice. She is a great mother, with a huge passion for our three children. Returning to work was not her preferred choice, to say the least. But the ministry is worth every effort, because it is part of our discipleship and our calling.

Promise

In verse 11, Jesus gave the promise: *"He who overcomes will not be hurt at all by the second death."* Yes, there is a second death which is much worse than the first. It is spiritual death resulting in eternal separation from God and every trace of goodness. Hell is no fun, no joke; it is real. I have heard some ignorantly say they will enjoy themselves with their friends in Hell. Unfortunately for them, even the tiniest bit of joy comes from the goodness of God, and in Hell there will not be the slightest hint of laughter. The Smyrnan Christians were assured that this is worse than martyrdom.

Conclusion

For the Christian, we can see the contrast between the heavenly perspective and the earthly one. The Smyrnan believers were poor, yet they were really rich. The Jews saw themselves as the people of God, yet they were a synagogue of Satan in Smyrna. Some Christians would die a martyr's death, but they are the ones who will receive the crown of life. What an irony!

What has been your outlook on life? When you look upon your circumstances, is yours a spiritual perspective? Will you pay the cost of faithfulness?

The key word for this letter is "faithfulness," even in the midst of suffering. What an inspiration this church is to us! They take Philippians 3:10 literally: *"I want to know Christ and the power of his resurrection and the sharing of his sufferings by becoming like him in his death"* (NRSV). Christ had no word of rebuke for this church! They were not bitter about their trying circumstances. They were effective in their witness — so much so that their lives were placed in danger. Their first love was intact in spite of all. They were faithful to the very end.

Questions for Private Study and Discussion

1. What might be a natural temptation for the Smyrnan Christians to experience, being poor in a wealthy city?

2. How is it that tribulation and trials come from the devil and not from God?

3. How do you handle personal trials?

4. What might it cost to be a faithful Christian in the twenty-first century?

5. What has obeying your ministry calling cost you?

Chapter 5

HOLINESS: THE MESSAGE TO THE CHURCH IN PERGAMUM

Revelation 2:12-17:

> "To the angel of the church in Pergamum write:
> These are the words of him who has the sharp, double-edged sword.
> {13} I know where you live — where Satan has his throne. Yet you
> remain true to my name. You did not renounce your faith in me, even
> in the days of Antipas, my faithful witness, who was put to death in
> your city — where Satan lives.
> {14} Nevertheless, I have a few things against you: You have peo-
> ple there who hold to the teaching of Balaam, who taught Balak to
> entice the Israelites to sin by eating food sacrificed to idols and by
> committing sexual immorality. {15} Likewise you also have those
> who hold to the teaching of the Nicolaitans. {16} Repent therefore!
> Otherwise, I will soon come to you and will fight against them with
> the sword of my mouth.
> {17} He who has an ear, let him hear what the Spirit says to the
> churches. To him who overcomes, I will give some of the hidden
> manna. I will also give him a white stone with a new name written
> on it, known only to him who receives it."

The key word for this church is "holiness." Holiness means more than
just sexual purity. It includes the important principle of consecration.
As we shall see, some in the church at Pergamum were struggling with
the issue of complete consecration.

This letter deals with a very powerful weapon of Satan, the weapon of
seduction. If the fear of martyrdom will not cause us to falter as Christians, the evil one will use his power of seduction. It has been an effective

strategy against believers throughout history. If killing Christians won't work, he will tempt, deceive and seduce them. Such was the situation faced by the Pergamum church. They were steadfast and immovable even when confronted by death, but some had given in to Satan's more subtle and deceitful ways.

Fortunately, Jesus has a weapon that is more than capable of solving the problem. The letter begins by stating that Christ comes with a sharp, double-edged sword. It is the sword of the Spirit, the Word capable of judging and of discerning truth from error. Hebrews 4:12 says that *"the word of God is living and active. Sharper than any double-edged sword, it penetrates even to dividing soul and spirit, joints and marrow; it judges the thoughts and attitudes of the heart."* It continues to say, in verse 13, that *"nothing in all creation is hidden from God's sight. Everything is uncovered and laid bare before the eyes of him to whom we must give account."* Christ's words have the power to unveil deception and cut away that which is false.

Christ's Commendation

In verse 13, we see that the Pergamum Christians received the award for remaining true to Christ's name in very difficult circumstances. If you recall, the churches at Ephesus and Smyrna were commended similarly. There is, however, a major difference between them and Pergamum. Pergamum is described as the city where Satan lived and had his throne: *"I know where you live — where Satan has his throne. Yet you remain true to my name."* Pergamum was the devil-worshipping center of Asia Minor in more ways than one.

The city of Pergamum had a multitude of heathen temples and four popular pagan cults, those of Asklepios, Zeus, Athena and Dionysus. Of these, the cults of Asklepios and Zeus were the most important. The symbol for Asklepios was a serpent, and people came from all over to be healed by the snake. Zeus, on the other hand, was worshiped by many as "the savior." Pergamum also had three temples dedicated to the emperor, and attained the title of "Temple-Sweeper" before Ephesus and Smyrna did. It was the center of worship for the emperor cult.

These were not the only reasons for Pergamum to be called the throne of Satan. There was something else of equal significance.

Holiness: The Message to the Church in Pergamum

Pergamum was the most important cultural center of the region, and was known as the "ancient seat of culture." It had the second largest library in the entire Roman Empire. Interestingly, the word *parchment* in English was derived from the word *Pergamum*. Pergamum would have been a haven for artists, writers and philosophers. It was a place where fresh new cultural ideas could originate and be popularized. Satan chose to establish his throne there.

This gives us an insight into how Lucifer works. His aim throughout history since the days of Adam and Eve has been to deceive and to destroy. His means for accomplishing his aim was through the promotion of an anti-God, anti-Christ popular culture. The challenge for the Pergamum Christians was to be in the world for Christ but not of the world. The challenge for us who live in the twenty-first-century postmodern West is to reach postmodern unbelievers for Christ without buying into their ethos, and to do so without falling into the other extreme — pharisaism or hyperfundamentalism.

It is easy for Christians to fall into either extreme. At one end is to overidentify with our culture to the extent that we lose our distinctiveness through compromise. But the other end is equally unproductive. We become so excessively cautious in not wanting to be influenced by the world that we withdraw from it. Then we attempt to maintain our purity by attacking and condemning everything that is in the world. It is worth remembering that the greatest enemy of Jesus while He was on earth was pharisaism. The Pharisees had a rigid and legalistic interpretation of Scripture that focused on a list of dos and don'ts. They missed the Messiah.

Satan had used the weapon of martyrdom on the church at Pergamum. Antipas, the faithful witness, had been killed. But as verse 13 notes, they were steadfast: *"You did not deny your faith in me even in the days of Antipas my witness, my faithful one, who was killed among you, where Satan lives"* (NRSV). Thus, as with the Christians at Smyrna, dying for the faith was not an issue for the Pergamum Christians. They would have willingly given their bodies to be burned. The devil had to change his strategy if he was to be successful in defeating this church.

Christ's Rebuke and Warning

Satan was gaining ground in the church through his strategy of seduction. Christ had to rebuke them in verse 14: *"Nevertheless, I have a few things against you: You have people there who hold to the teaching of Balaam, who taught Balak to entice the Israelites to sin by eating food sacrificed to idols and by committing sexual immorality."* What was the teaching of Balaam, and who was Balak?

Balak was the king of Moab who wanted to destroy Israel. In Numbers 22 to 25, we read that King Balak wanted to hire the "prophet" Balaam to put a curse on Israel. Balaam agreed, but every time he opened his mouth to curse Israel, blessings came out instead. The Spirit of the Lord would not allow His people to be cursed. Finally, inspired by Satan, Balaam thought up a strategy that would help the king destroy Israel. Balaam taught Balak to entice the people of Israel to sin through idolatry and sexual immorality with some Moabite women. This succeeded, and as a result, the judgment of God fell on Israel, and 24,000 Israelites died in a plague. Balak had succeeded through the strategy of seduction.

The apostle Peter mentioned Balaam in his second epistle. The Christians he was writing to were in danger of falling into the same trap. He warned his flock against Balaamites. In 2 Peter 2:13-19, eight characteristics of Balaamites can be identified:

- They revel in their pleasure (verse13).
- They seduce the unstable (verse 14).
- They are experts in greed (verse 14).
- They love the benefits of wickedness (verse 15).
- They are arrogant and boastful (verse 18).
- They appeal to lustful desires (verse 18).
- They entice new Christians (verse 18).
- They are slaves of depravity (verse19).

It is worth remembering that Peter was describing Christians who have fallen into Balaam's trap. They are like a dog that returns to its vomit, and even their salvation is in question (2 Peter 2:20-22). The issue here is not unbelievers being enslaved by the world, but rather believers being enslaved. They were like the Israelites who were seduced by Balaam and Balak. We must not make the mistake of judging unbelievers with these verses in Second Peter. Unbelievers belong to the world because they have never been saved. They are not yet part of the Kingdom of God. These verses were targeted at Balaamite Christians, who are in a more precarious condition because they have tasted salvation.

Important to note, too, is that the Balaamite characteristics described in Second Peter do *not* refer to Christians genuinely struggling with sin. Balaamite Christians have given up struggling and have given in to sin. They knowingly love their sinful lifestyle. Furthermore, they entice other believers to join them. For instance, they do not struggle with greed, but rather are "experts in greed." They do not confess their sins and ask for forgiveness (see 1 John 1:9), but boast about them instead.

Jude picked up on a similar theme: *"Woe to them! They have taken the way of Cain; they have rushed for profit into Balaam's error; they have been destroyed in Korah's rebellion"* (Jude 11). Cain succumbed to jealousy, Balaam gave in to greed, and Korah was consumed by the lust for power. These were supposed to be God's people.

Ultimately, it was Satan who won the battle against God's people in Numbers 22 to 25. Balaam was after money, Balak was after political power, but Satan was out to destroy God's chosen ones. The devil aimed to ruin God's salvation of mankind by destroying God's people.

So, Jesus gave the church at Pergamum a stern warning: *"Repent therefore! Otherwise, I will soon come to you and will fight against them with the sword of my mouth"* (verse 16). Judgment will surely follow if they do not repent. Matthew 18:7 is worth remembering here, where Jesus said, *"Woe to the world because of the things that cause people to sin! Such things must come, but woe to the man through whom they come!"* A little leaven leavens the whole lump.

Unfortunately, Balaamites are increasing in the twenty-first -century Western church. Some are more obvious than others. For instance, there are some who advocate that homosexuality is an acceptable lifestyle, even for the clergy! Some churches would even openly promote this. But perhaps it is the more subtle temptations that are of the greatest danger to evangelical Christians.

Several practical lessons can be gleaned from this letter to the church at Pergamum. Two will be highlighted here. First, Satan is the greatest seducer. He wants to enslave us again to the principles of this world. He wants us to be tempted and trapped by such snares as jealousy, greed and lust. He wants us to be enslaved by pleasure and to rob us of the simple enjoyment of it. Second, he wants us to go one step further by becoming Balaamites. He wants us to advocate sin to others and to entice unsuspecting believers. He wants us to become seducers like himself.

Reward

As in all the letters to the seven churches, there is a reward for those who overcome. *"To him who overcomes, I will give some of the hidden manna. I will also give him a white stone with a new name written on it, known only to him who receives it"* (verse 17). "Hidden manna" possibly refers to heavenly bread, which denotes salvation. "White stone" points to the blessing of legal acquittal, or "justification." "A new name" alludes to a new nature and new citizenship in the Kingdom of God.

The challenge for the church at Pergamum is to be holy as God is holy. The word *holy* in the original language means "to be set apart." Central to holiness is the principle of consecration, the dedication of oneself fully for the use of God. We as Christians are set apart for the Kingdom of God and for the service of His Kingdom. Balaam's teaching seeks to lure us back into the world through seduction and thus nullify our effectiveness for the Kingdom. But there can be no compromises in this matter. The call for the Pergamum Christians then, as it is for us now, is to be holy as He is holy.

Questions for Private Study and Discussion

1. What similarities might the culture of the city of Pergamum have with the culture of your city?

2. What is the teaching of Balaam?

3. How can Christians avoid the two extremes mentioned in this chapter (compromise and pharisaism)?

4. Describe in your own words two practical lessons mentioned in this chapter. Give some examples.

5. What is holiness, and why was it an issue for the Pergamum church?

Chapter 6

TRUTH: THE MESSAGE TO THE CHURCH IN THYATIRA

Revelation 2:18-29:

"To the angel of the church in Thyatira write:
These are the words of the Son of God, whose eyes are like blazing
fire and whose feet are like burnished bronze. {19} I know your
deeds, your love and faith, your service and perseverance, and that
you are now doing more than you did at first.

{20} Nevertheless, I have this against you: You tolerate that woman
Jezebel, who calls herself a prophetess. By her teaching she misleads
my servants into sexual immorality and the eating of food sacrificed
to idols. {21} I have given her time to repent of her immorality, but
she is unwilling. {22} So I will cast her on a bed of suffering, and
I will make those who commit adultery with her suffer intensely,
unless they repent of her ways. {23} I will strike her children dead.
Then all the churches will know that I am he who searches hearts
and minds, and I will repay each of you according to your deeds.
{24} Now I say to the rest of you in Thyatira, to you who do not hold
to her teaching and have not learned Satan's so-called deep secrets
(I will not impose any other burden on you): {25} Only hold on to
what you have until I come.

{26} To him who overcomes and does my will to the end, I will give
authority over the nations —

{27} 'He will rule them with an iron scepter; he will dash them to
pieces like pottery' — just as I have received authority from my
Father. {28} I will also give him the morning star. {29} He who
has an ear, let him hear what the Spirit says to the churches."

The key word for this letter is "truth." The *Jezebel* at Thyatira was a false prophetess misleading believers through her false teaching. Believers in the twenty-first century need to know how to discern truth from error — they need to know the Word of God. Otherwise, they will be led astray by false teachers whom the Lord has warned will surely attempt to infiltrate the Church. The Bible is our greatest safeguard against error. But it needs to be understood and correctly taught.

It is encouraging that Jesus wrote the longest of the seven letters to the least well known of all the seven cities. Thyatira was a city with no illustrious history and which played no significant part in recorded Church history. Yet Jesus wrote the longest letter to them. In His eyes all churches everywhere are equally important, and He pays equal attention to all. There is no measure of prejudice in the penetrating eyes of God. Everyone is a sinner in need of salvation. His grace is no respecter of persons, whether they are rich or poor, young or old, black or white.

The letter begins by reminding us that "*these are the words of the Son of God.*" It was really Jesus' word to the churches, not John's. To His people in Thyatira, Jesus described Himself as one "*whose eyes are like blazing fire and whose feet are like burnished bronze.*" This is a clear reminder that nothing about the Church escapes His penetrating gaze. His X-ray vision sees all, including that which goes on within our heart of hearts. This is why He was able to "know their deeds" (verse 19), both the good and the bad. His feet described as like burnished bronze remind us of His eternal and unshakable rule over all, establishing the permanent Kingdom of God. The reward for the Thyatiran Christians is that they will share in His reign (see verse 26), if they remain faithful! It is a privilege not worth sacrificing for the type of short term earthly gain that Jezebel was engaged in. It is also a reminder that we His servants are accountable to Him and He does demand an account, as evidenced in this letter.

Commendations From the Son of God

Jesus gave this church five commendations: for their deeds, love, faith, service and perseverance. Deeds here would have included everything they did, including their occupation, or work. In the context of Thyatira, this would have involved the popular business activities of buying and selling. Thyatira was characterized by her trade, and in particular, by the purple garments for which she was famous. Lydia, one of Paul's well-known converts, was a Thyatiran businesswoman in the clothing industry: *"One of those listening was a woman named Lydia, a dealer in purple cloth from the city of Thyatira, who was a worshiper of God. The Lord opened her heart to respond to Paul's message"* (Acts 16:14). It is no small thing for Jesus to commend them for their good works, faith and service in a compromising business environment involving trade guilds. The practice of emperor worship was closely tied to the guilds.

In addition to these five commendations, Jesus gave them a bonus which set this church apart from the others. To the Thyatiran church, He said: *"You are now doing more than you did at first."* They were adding to the fruit they were already bearing. Peter wrote of the importance of growing in fruitfulness in 2 Peter 1:5-8, *"For this very reason, make every effort to ADD to your faith goodness; and to goodness, knowledge; and to knowledge, self-control; and to self-control, perseverance; and to perseverance, godliness; and to godliness, brotherly kindness; and to brotherly kindness, love. For if you possess these qualities in INCREASING MEASURE, they will keep you from being ineffective and unproductive in your knowledge of our Lord Jesus Christ."*

This is surely an example for us to follow: to be growing in fruitfulness rather than be diminishing in zeal. It would be useful to ask ourselves: "Am I more effective now as a Christian than five years ago? Is the fruit of the Spirit more evident in my life now compared to five years ago?" The fruit of perseverance, for which the Thyatirans were commended, is a vital quality necessary for long-term effectiveness.

Jesus' Rebuke

In the next section Jesus offered a life-giving rebuke to the church. It had to do with a woman named Jezebel who was leading believers into idolatry and sexual immorality by her false teaching. Jezebel was probably not her real name, but she was called that due to her similarity to the Old Testament Jezebel. In 1 Kings 18:4, we read that Jezebel, King Ahab's wife, was killing off the Lord's prophets. Even Elijah fled for his life in fear because of her. She was shrewd and idolatrous, and she eventually died a gruesome death as prophesied in 1 Kings 21:23:

"And also concerning Jezebel the Lord says: 'Dogs will devour Jezebel by the wall of Jezreel.' "

Similarly, the Thyatiran Jezebel was a dangerous person to leave uncorrected and undisciplined. One of the key issues was her false teaching (see Revelation 2:21 and 24) that was leading other believers into sin. Christians in this church were being gradually led astray by a deficiency of biblical truth. This highlights the dangers of false teaching and the importance of true instruction.

Why is sound biblical teaching so important? One reason is that an effective way to deal with false teaching is to ensure that believers are well-grounded in teaching that is scriptural. Once they are grounded in Scripture, they will be able to evaluate any teaching that crosses their path. The best medicine against error is truth. Another reason is that there is an indisputable connection between our thinking and our behavior. If we do not think biblically, we will have difficulty behaving in a Christian manner. Even secular psychologists recognize the influence of thinking on behavior, as evidenced by an entire discipline called cognitive-behavioral therapy. Our cognition (thought) influences our emotion and behavior. Jezebel was demonstrating this at Thyatira. Her false teaching was leading believers into immorality and idolatry.

The kind of truth needed at Thyatira was biblical truth. The Bible is the Word of God. God has spoken, through the Scriptures — the Old and New Testaments. Imagine reading on the front page of the newspaper: "God has spoken." It would surely capture the attention of many people. "What did God say?" Well, God has indeed spoken — through the written Word.

It is not sufficient to just know the Word of God in fragments. We need to know the fullness of His Word. In Acts 20:27, when Paul was saying farewell to the elders of the Ephesian church, he declared that he had taught them *the whole will of God.*" Then he concluded by saying, *"Now I commit you to God and to the word of his grace, which can build you up and give you an inheritance among all those who are sanctified"* (verse 32). Knowing the fullness of God's Word will protect Christians from three dangers. First is the peril of being deceived by "savage wolves." This is the danger facing the Thyatiran church. Second is the peril of building our lives and ministries on an emphasis, for example, emphasizing the importance of signs and wonders so much that the role of suffering is neglected (note that the reverse can also be true). Third is the peril of omission. We can omit an important teaching in the Bible, for instance, the Great Commission.

It has been said that in Australia and in the West there are four kinds of Christian teachers and preachers. First, there are those who don't believe the Bible and don't use it. Second, there are those who don't believe the Bible but do use it. Third, there are those who believe the Bible but don't use it. Fourth, there are those who believe the Bible and use it. The Thyatiran church needed teachers in this fourth category.

In the ministry of Living Impact, in addition to church planting, we emphasize the need to teach new believers the Word of God. In fact, I have designed a complete leadership course to facilitate this important process. Understanding the Word of God requires an investment of time and effort. There is no shortcut. For the Word of God to become a part of us demands energy and sacrifice. It involves more than just reading the Word, because it is possible to read without comprehension. It might involve committing ourselves to a good Bible course or systematically listening to some good Bible-teaching tapes. The fact is that anything worthwhile requires an investment of time and effort. How much more the understanding of God's eternal Word.

Jesus' Warning

In the next section Jesus issued a stern warning. He had given Jezebel time to repent, but she had not done so. Therefore, the last warning is that unless she and her followers repent, they will be judged and disciplined. However, it is the patience of Jesus that should be noted first. God is not a faultfinder seeking for opportunities to condemn us. Yet He will not allow us to perpetually live in sin, especially of the kind Jezebel was engaged in.

The tragedy is that Jezebel will not repent. It is not that she cannot, but that she *will* not. Repentance is of the will. It involves making a decision to change course, to make a U-turn so to speak. It begins by recognizing that one is traveling in the wrong direction and ends with one deciding to go the right way. It has nothing to do with feelings or whether one wants to. It is a matter of the will. As a song writer put it: "You want to, but will you?" Jezebel would not.

Accountability

Jesus continued in verse 23: "*I will strike her children dead. Then all the churches will know that I am he who searches hearts and minds, and I will repay each of you according to your deeds.*" The word *children* here refers to followers. Judgment will fall not only upon Jezebel but upon her disciples. God will hold them accountable and repay them according to their deeds.

Worthy of emphasis here is that we are accountable to God as servants of Christ. It is to the triumphant resurrected Lord that we must give account. To Thyatira, He was described as having eyes like blazing fire. Nothing escapes His penetrating gaze. He perceives the deepest secrets of our hearts and discerns our motives. We cannot hide anything from Him, so it is pointless to try. It is also foolish to try to hide it from ourselves. He *"searches hearts and minds,"* and if we will listen to the Spirit, He will convict us of sin.

Fortunately for us, His grace and forgiveness are always available to those who will repent. This was true even for Jezebel, who was not only living in sin but instructing others to do likewise.

The Promise to Rule

In the concluding verses, Jesus tells the Thyatiran Christians that it is not worth sacrificing their eternal inheritance for the sake of ungodly temporal gain: "*To him who overcomes and does my will to the end, I will give authority over the nations*" (verse 26). Christ Himself has been given this authority to reign over all by the Father (verse 27), and those who persevere will reign with Him. What a promise! To Jezebel and her followers, such an eternal unshakable promise is worth the repentance it takes. The One whose feet are like burnished bronze reminds them of the nature of His Kingdom and rule — unshakable and permanent. All who hold on till the end will be part of it.

Truth: The Message to the Church in Thyatira

This is a great encouragement for us living in the twenty-first century. We too will reign with Him in an unchanging Kingdom if we remain faithful. No temporal gain is worth the sacrifice of such a promise. We are to adopt long-term — eternal term — thinking. Governments around the world that promote superannuation encourage long-term saving and investment, for the sake of our own retirements. The scriptural perspective extends that line of thought to the spiritual eternal realm. It makes logical sense. Those who invest in the stock market are often encouraged to adopt a long-term perspective. Similarly, Christians who make an eternal investment are to think beyond the volatility and impermanence of this present life.

Questions for Private Study and Discussion

1. The key word for this letter is "truth." Why is teaching important when it comes to biblical truth?

2. How much of the Bible do you understand, and what can you do to further your grasp of the Word?

3. The Thyatiran Christians were commended for doing more than they did at first. How can you ensure that the same is true of you in five years' time?

4. In what ways does God hold us accountable in our lives and ministries?

5. What are the things that might prevent Christians from receiving the promise Christ gave in verse 26?

Chapter 7

WATCHFULNESS: THE MESSAGE TO THE CHURCH IN SARDIS

Revelation 3:1-6:

> "To the angel of the church in Sardis write:
> These are the words of him who holds the seven spirits of God and the seven stars. I know your deeds; you have a reputation of being alive, but you are dead. {2} Wake up! Strengthen what remains and is about to die, for I have not found your deeds complete in the sight of my God. {3} Remember, therefore, what you have received and heard; obey it, and repent. But if you do not wake up, I will come like a thief, and you will not know at what time I will come to you. {4} Yet you have a few people in Sardis who have not soiled their clothes. They will walk with me, dressed in white, for they are worthy. {5} He who overcomes will, like them, be dressed in white. I will never blot out his name from the book of life, but will acknowledge his name before my Father and his angels. {6} He who has an ear, let him hear what the Spirit says to the churches."

The key word for this letter is "watchfulness." The church at Sardis was slumbering. She needed to wake up, stay awake and keep watch. She needed to realize that her false reputation was blinding her to the truth of her spiritual condition.

There are a few important differences worth noting between the Sardisian church and the previous churches we have considered. First, those needing a rebuke in this church were the majority. For the other churches, such as Thyatira and Pergamum, it was the minority who were in trouble. Second, there was no persecution for the church at Sardis. Third, there was no problem with heresies.

Given that there were no heresies and persecution faced by the church, one might wonder what the problem with this church was. In the absence of those internal and external stressors, the church ought to have been thriving and forging ahead. Instead, they had a crisis worse than that encountered by the other churches we have so far considered. The main issue is that they were spiritually dead. Such was the pronouncement of Jesus.

Jesus is described here as One who *"has the seven spirits of God and the seven stars"* (NRSV). The *"seven spirits"* described here and elsewhere in Revelation depict the Holy Spirit. This by no means diminishes the divinity of the Holy Spirit as the Third Person of the trinity, but rather it highlights the ministry of the Spirit in the Church on earth. As Michael Wilcock comments: "Christ can bring both the church and the Spirit together in renewal." The church at Sardis needed an awakening from their spiritual slumber and Christ had the power to renew them (including their leadership: seven "stars") through His representative, the Holy Spirit.

Jesus' Assessment

Jesus said to the church, in verse 1, *"I know your deeds; you have a reputation of being alive, but you are dead."* Their activities and works were known to Jesus, but His assessment of them was not good. The verdict of the Author of Life was that they were spiritually dead. As if that was not bad enough, their condition was even worse than death.

The saddest aspect about this church was not that they were spiritually dead, but that they did not even know it. Without an awareness of their true spiritual condition, they would not be seeking for a cure. If one is aware of contracting a deadly disease, a course of remedy might be pursued. Without that awareness, it might one day be too late for any successful remedy. Spiritually, the church at Sardis was dangerously infected, and they were not aware of it.

Their spiritual condition was compounded by the fact that they had a false reputation of being alive. They thought they were healthy and well. They were blinded by a false reputation for the exact opposite of their true condition. Jesus declared: *"I have not found your deeds complete in the sight of my God"* (verse 2). There was a great discrepancy between the perception of others and the perception of God. People thought the church was alive and well, perhaps even worthy of imitation. But God thought they were a dead church. Their good name was preventing them from recognizing the reality of their condition. Perhaps one deceiving factor for the church was that they did possess some good deeds, but the deeds were not complete. It was not as though they had no deeds whatsoever. They might even have been an activity-driven church, since they had the appearance of being alive. However, external activity may not be a good measure of internal spirituality.

Having served as a pastor for ten years, I confess that it is possible to encounter such situations in the church today. A church may have the reputation of being alive. Outsiders might say, "Oh, that's a great church." A church might give the appearance of life by her many programs and activities. She might even be a large church in terms of the size of the congregation. The building might even look fabulous. Yet the assessment of Jesus could be entirely different from their earthly reputation. This is not a criticism of large churches in itself. The same can be said of small churches. The real issue is not church size but church health.

Rebuke and Remedy

The command Jesus gave them was *"Wake up! Strengthen what remains and is about to die ..."* (verse 2). They were to awaken from their slumber. Fortunately, there was still hope. All was not lost. There still remained some signs of life, and they were to strengthen whatever little was left. They could be resuscitated and revived if they would wake up and come to their senses. This clearly demonstrates that renewal is a combination of divine initiative and human response. Christ had approached them and has spoken the word to them. They were to respond with obedience.

Worth noting here is that the Greek word translated *"wake up"* is also the word for "be watchful" or "be vigilant." It is translated *"keep watch"* in Matthew 24:42: *"Therefore KEEP WATCH, because you do not know on what day your Lord will come,"* and in Matthew 26:38: *"Then he said to them, 'My soul is overwhelmed with sorrow to the point of death. Stay here and KEEP WATCH with me.' "* In Matthew 26:41 the same word is used:

"WATCH and pray so that you will not fall into temptation. The spirit is willing, but the body is weak." In Acts 20:31 and 1 Corinthians 16:13 in the NIV it is translated *"be on your guard."* In 1 Thessalonians 5:6 and in 1 Peter 5:8 it is *"alert."* These words were all appropriate for the church at Sardis. They were to "wake up," "be watchful," "be on guard," and "be alert." Interestingly, the same advice would also have been appropriate for the city of Sardis.

The church at Sardis was behaving just like their city. Sardis was well known for its pride, its presumptuous arrogance and its slackness in defense. It was the first center to mint gold and silver coinage. Its leader, Croesus, became a legend for his riches and his arrogance. Twice the city was attacked unawares because they placed no guards at their point of strength — the side built on a vertical rock. Unfortunately, the culture of the city had seeped into the church. It should have been the reverse, the church influencing its city with the Gospel.

For the church to wake up, Jesus commanded them to do three things. First, they were to remember what they had received and heard. This would be the Gospel and any related teaching the apostles have given. This is the Word of God. Second, they were to obey what they had heard. To hear the Word and persistently refuse to obey would result in apathy. As in the days of Amos, it would result in a famine of the Word in which God would no longer speak to them through the prophets. Yes, Israel in the days of Amos still had the written Scriptures of the Torah, but God no longer spoke to them through the prophets. Third, they were to awaken from their slumber.

Warning

The second half of verse 3 gives us the consequence of not being vigilant: *"But if you do not wake up, I will come like a thief, and you will not know at what time I will come to you."* It is possible that this referred to the Second Coming. If so, it would be a very rude awakening if they were not ready. However, from the benefit of hindsight, Christ was probably not referring to His Second Coming with regard to the church at Sardis.

The warning most likely referred to a special visitation of Jesus in the power of the Spirit. This also makes sense in the context of verse 1 where

Jesus specifically mentioned the "seven spirits," the Holy Spirit. In any case, it would be a rude awakening for them if they were unprepared. The Second Coming would no doubt be the most frightening and spectacular. But a great manifestation of the Spirit's power could also make for a tremendous shock to the slumbering.

The idea here is that it would be too late for the church if she was not prepared for the visitation of Jesus. If it was the Second Coming, judgment immediately follows. If it was a special manifestation of the Spirit, judgment usually accompanies such events. Ananias and Sapphira in Acts 5 would be a spectacular example of such. In the meantime, Jesus is speaking the word to them through the Spirit in this letter. He who has an ear, let him hear. Whichever is the case, the consequence is clear: Those who will not waken to the whisper of the Spirit will be rudely awakened by the blast of His trumpet.

The word for us is the same. We too need to wake up if we are slumbering. The Spirit is whispering His word to us now: Keep watch and be vigilant. Repent if necessary and obey His Word. Remember that we are not our own. We are bought with a price — that of His own precious blood. Strengthen what remains and be alert. One good way to keep watch is to climb the "watchtower" of private prayer and devotion as the prophet Habakkuk did.

Commendation to the Worthy

Christ did give the church a commendation, but not to the majority: *"Yet you have a few people in Sardis who have not soiled their clothes. They will walk with me, dressed in white, for they are worthy"* (verse 4). The phrases *soiled their clothes* and *dressed in white* are worthy of comment in this context. We know that they do not refer to sexual immorality or to the worship of idols, since Christ did not rebuke this church for these things as He did Pergamum. Yet by His comments it is clear that the majority in the church did soil their clothes.

If the two phrases did not refer to sexual immorality or to ancient idolatry, what did they refer to? Most likely it had to do with what Christ rebuked them for, which was their spiritual slumber. They were spiritually asleep and thus were not walking in a worthy manner. This is also a clear example of a church that has compromised on holiness by not fulfilling the purposes of the Kingdom. By the standards set by the city of Sardis, the church was "worldly." To be worldly is to be unholy. Holiness is more than mere sexual purity.

Reward

There is a reward for those who are worthy and those who will repent: *"He who overcomes will, like them, be dressed in white. I will never blot out his name from the book of life, but will acknowledge his name before my Father and his angels"* (verse 5). This was a clear encouragement and incentive for those who were slumbering to wake up. They were to overcome their drowsiness. The reward will be to have Christ acknowledge their names before the Father and the angels.

They could either have a reputation among men on earth or among angels in Heaven. One would be a false reputation that is temporal, the other a genuine name that is eternal. The choice for them and us ought to be simple. Better to have our names acknowledged by the Father than to sacrifice that for a false reputation among men.

Questions for Private Study and Discussion

1. Why is it important to be spiritually watchful, and how can one maintain a state of alertness?

2. In what ways can a false reputation blind us to the truth? How do we prevent ourselves from falling into this trap?

3. If you were to meet your Savior tomorrow, would you be ready? How can you prepare yourself?

4. What are the symptoms of spiritual slumber? In other words, how do we know if we are spiritually asleep?

Chapter 8

"KINGPORTUNITY": THE MESSAGE TO THE CHURCH IN PHILADELPHIA

Revelation 3:7-13
"To the angel of the church in Philadelphia write:
These are the words of him who is holy and true, who holds the key
of David. What he opens no one can shut, and what he shuts no one
can open. {8} I know your deeds. See, I have placed before you an
open door that no one can shut. I know that you have little strength,
yet you have kept my word and have not denied my name. {9} I will
make those who are of the synagogue of Satan, who claim to be Jews
though they are not, but are liars — I will make them come and fall
down at your feet and acknowledge that I have loved you. {10} Since
you have kept my command to endure patiently, I will also keep you
from the hour of trial that is going to come upon the whole world to
test those who live on the earth.
{11} I am coming soon. Hold on to what you have, so that no one
will take your crown. {12} Him who overcomes I will make a pillar
in the temple of my God. Never again will he leave it. I will write
on him the name of my God and the name of the city of my God, the
new Jerusalem, which is coming down out of heaven from my God;
and I will also write on him my new name. {13} He who has an ear,
let him hear what the Spirit says to the churches."

The key word for the letter to the Philadelphian church is "kingportunity." Yes, it is a word we would not find in any English dictionary. I have joined together the words *kingdom* and *opportunity* to form the word "kingportunity." Originally I wanted to use the word "opportunity," but it is not just any opportunity that is being referred to. I definitely want to avoid the negative aspect of "opportunism" or of one who is "opportunistic" at all costs. I am certainly not referring to the self-centered kind of opportunity for self-interest or self-promotion. This is a specific kind of opportunity — a Kingdom opportunity. It is God opening doors of opportunity for service in His Kingdom. It is ministry opportunity for the extension of the Kingdom of God. This is what is referred to in the letter to the church at Philadelphia.

If I were to select my favorite church out of the seven churches in Revelation, this would be it. The church at Philadelphia is one of two churches that did not receive any rebuke from Jesus. But it is not for this reason alone that I choose it as my most favored. "Perfection" is not one of my criteria. My main reason for nominating Philadelphia is that they were living up to their potential for the Kingdom of God. They were being the kind of people God was calling them to be — both in character and in ministry. They were seizing the opportunities God was giving them for the Kingdom. Furthermore, they were doing this in spite of their *"little strength"* (verse 8). The church at Philadelphia is the only one that survived through history to this day. It even survived the Muslim invasion of the city in a later century.

There are three main lessons this letter can teach us. First, we Christians are citizens of God's Kingdom. Second, Christ can open for us any door of opportunity for ministry in His Kingdom. Third, we are to hold on to our Kingdom citizenship regardless of circumstances. Let us explore these precious truths and principles for effective living.

We Are Citizens of the Kingdom of God

Yes, we may be citizens of the United States, of Australia, or of any country in the world, but we are first and foremost citizens of the Kingdom of God. Our country of birth, our nationality and our ethnic origins are important, but they are secondary factors for the Christian. This might be hard to swallow for Americans after the terrible tragedy of September 11. But the Christian should view himself or herself primarily as a citizen of Heaven. Yes, we should obey the laws of the land and be good earthly citizens, but above and beyond that we are primarily of God's Kingdom. It is unfortunate that some Christians view this in the reverse. They put their nationality above their spirituality. They place the temporal above the eternal. They see the brotherhood of race as more important than the brotherhood of Jesus. And so, history has shown that some would war against other Christians because of their ethnicity.

The Kingdom of God is a theme that runs throughout the letter to the church at Philadelphia. Revelation 3:7 tells us that *these are the words of him who is holy and true, who holds the key of David. What he opens no one can shut, and what he shuts no one can open.* Whatever this key is, it is very important. It is the key of David. The door that it opens no man can shut. So, what is this key of David and what is it that it opens and shuts? The answer is not difficult to discern. Put simply, the key of David is the key to the house of David, and the house of David is the Kingdom of God. Thus the key of David is the key to the Kingdom, and the door it opens is the door into the Kingdom of God. For those who may be in doubt, let me remind you that Jesus the Messiah is the son of David who sits on his throne forever. The messianic Kingdom is the spiritual Davidic kingdom. The Davidic Covenant is the fulfillment of the Abrahamic Covenant, and all Christians are children of Abraham.

This was very important to the Philadelphian Christians. They were shut out from the Jewish synagogues in the city. Now in the letter Jesus assured them that though they were excluded from the synagogues they were included in the Kingdom of God. They were the true children of David, and of Abraham.

Jesus went further, in verse 9, to say that *"I will make those who are of the synagogue of Satan, who claim to be Jews though they are not, but are liars — I will make them come and fall down at your feet and acknowledge that I have loved you."* This represented a real insult to the Jews of Philadelphia, who saw themselves as the people of God. Yet Jesus declared them to be of the synagogue of Satan. According to Jesus, they were not the true Jews. The point is that the true Jew is not one by race or genealogy but by spiritual inheritance. Only Christians are the true people of God, genuine children of Abraham. I understand that in a pluralistic world, this is difficult to proclaim without someone being offended.

This is our true biblical heritage. All who are Christians are now the true "Jews" in that we are the children of God. This is not anti-Semitism, since any Jew by race can become a Christian. It is saying that race does not matter when it comes to the Kingdom of God. Gentiles are now included. This is the true understanding of scripture regarding the Abrahamic covenant. This is the Christian heritage traced to the promise God made to Abraham in Genesis 12. This was Paul's understanding in Ephesians 2:18-22: *"For through him we both have access to the Father by one Spirit. Consequently, you are no longer foreigners and aliens, but fellow citizens with God's people and members of God's household, built on the foundation of the apostles and prophets, with Christ Jesus himself as the chief cornerstone. In him the whole building is joined together and rises to become a holy temple in the Lord. And in him you too are being built together to become a dwelling in which God lives by his Spirit."* Peter makes this same point in 1 Peter 2:9, *"But you are a chosen people, a royal priesthood, a holy nation, a people belonging to God, that you may declare the praises of him who called you out of darkness into his wonderful light."*

As if that assurance was not enough, Jesus went on to say that He will write on the Philadelphian Christians *"the name of my God and the name of the city of my God, the new Jerusalem, which is coming down out of heaven from my God; and I will also write on him my new name"* (verse 12). The new Jerusalem is a spiritual city that comes from Heaven. The earthly Jerusalem bears no relevance beyond this age. A *"new name"* signifies the final seal of their new citizenship.

This is a great reminder to us that earth is not our home. We are indeed sojourners in this land. We are merely passing through as pilgrims. Have you ever had a nagging feeling inside that something is lacking on earth even when things are going well for you circumstantially? Yes, this may be true even for the committed, renewed Christian who enjoys the presence of God in worship. Why is that? It is because earth is not our home no matter how comfortable we make it. Paul experienced that when he said he longed to be with Jesus when death came. Perhaps Martin Luther experienced that too when he wrote, "I would not give one moment of Heaven for all the joys and riches of the world, even if it lasted for thousands and thousands of years."

Christ Can Open Any Door of Opportunity

In verse 8, Jesus said, *"See, I have placed before you an open door that no one can shut."* This is the door of service. This represents the open door of ministry that relates to the Kingdom of God. As I have mentioned earlier, the key that opens it is the key of David, which is the key to the Kingdom. The Philadelphian Christians were already citizens of the Kingdom. Now they were to extend that invitation to others. The Gospel must be spread to the ends of the earth.

Philadelphia was a city at a strategic location in terms of trade routes. It was a Hellenistic outpost. It was a "missionary" city, not for the promotion of the Gospel but for the advancement of Greek culture to the region, particularly Lydia and Phrygia. That was why in 5 A.D. it was known as "Little Athens." It was also called a "gateway to the east." It was to the church located in this city that Jesus said, *"I have placed before you an open door that no one can shut."* The church was to turn the city into a true missionary city for the Gospel.

It seemed as if the church was beginning to take hold of this "kingportunity." Jesus did not rebuke them for not doing so. Neither did our Lord have to urge them to seize the opportunity. It appears that Christ was encouraging them to keep doing what they were doing in spite of their *"little strength."* The church may have lacked physical resources. It may not have been a large church. It may have lacked political influence. But it had spiritual power and "patient endurance."

There are so many ways we can make an impact for the Kingdom these days. If there was ever a time for creativity and courage to take hold of God's opportunity, it is now. The global village seems to be shrinking by the year due to advances in technology, aviation and communication. The Internet has facilitated communication across national boundaries like never before. World missions are now more doable than ever. Christians can truly get involved to complete the task of world evangelization. This is why I am involved in a global mission ministry called "Living Impact." Our aim is to plant churches within the "10/40 Window," among the poorest and most unevangelized nations of the world. People from western countries are encouraged to sponsor *indigenous* church planters and visit the churches that are planted through short-term trips. We have church planters in both Burma (Myanmar) and India. Many are being saved. We believe the Lord has opened for us a huge door of opportunity. I have not come across a more cost-effective way of doing missions. For those interested, you can find out more from our website: www.livingimpact.org.

The challenge is for Christians living in the twenty-first century to put their creative energies to work — for the Kingdom. It requires initiative, vision and perseverance. But Christ can open any door for service. Brother Andrew's ministry since 1955 to the closed communist countries of the world is a great example. Christ opened a door for him that no human government can shut.

We need many more Christian philanthropists for the Kingdom, even if they do not have incredible wealth like the Bill Gateses and the Warren Buffets. This is because Christian ministry needs financial resources. I believe God has supplied the wealth for ministry, but some of it is tied up in the hip pockets of believers. Some Christians say, "I would give to God and the Kingdom if I had a lot of money." But the truth is if we are not giving now, we are not likely to give when we have more. It is not good enough to say, "If God blesses me with a million, I will give a hundred thousand." That is only a mere tithe, a mere starting point. Perhaps God will open the door for some Christians to be truly wealthy if they are willing to live on a hundred thousand and give nine hundred thousand away! Christian philanthropists don't have to be rich. They can be average middle class income earners. After all, those in the church at Philadelphia had *"little strength"* of their own, but they were seizing the "kingportunity." I enjoy sharing the testimony of a single woman who is a foreign missionary. She struggled to raise enough funds for herself, yet she chose to sponsor an indigenous church planter with Living Impact. I call that faith in action of the Macedonian caliber: *"Out of the most severe trial, their overflowing joy and their extreme poverty welled up in rich generosity"* (2 Corinthians 8:2).

We Must Hold On to Our Kingdom Citizenship

Verse 11 says, *"I am coming soon. Hold on to what you have, so that no one will take your crown."* This crown represents the victory prize for those who hold on to the end. They have received Kingdom citizenship by becoming Christians. Now they are to hang on to it more than to their lives. The reason is that Satan wants to snatch it away. The devil can do so only if they let him. Therefore, they were to hold on firmly. The same applies to us. We, too, must hold on to our Kingdom citizenship.

Their reward is further described in verse 12: *"Him who overcomes I will make a pillar in the temple of my God. Never again will he leave it. I will write on him the name of my God and the name of the city of my God, the new Jerusalem, which is coming down out of heaven from my God; and I will also write on him my new name."* To be made a pillar in the new Temple means to be made a permanent part of God's new society. This is God's promise to those who remain faithful and who are overcomers.

Questions for Private Study and Discussion

1. What does it mean to say that our citizenship in Heaven is more important than that on earth?

2. What does it mean, both theologically and practically, to be in the Kingdom of God?

3. Why was the church at Philadelphia such a great church?

4. What does "kingportunity" mean, and how is it different from any type of "opportunity"?

5. What doors has God opened for you at present?

6. What are some of the ways in which you can be engaged in "missions" in the twenty-first century?

7. In what ways can this chapter make a difference in your life this week?

Chapter 9

ZEAL: THE MESSAGE TO THE CHURCH IN LAODICEA

Revelation 3:14-22:

"To the angel of the church in Laodicea write:
These are the words of the Amen, the faithful and true witness, the
ruler of God's creation. {15} I know your deeds, that you are neither
cold nor hot. I wish you were either one or the other! {16} So, because
you are lukewarm — neither hot nor cold — I am about to spit you
out of my mouth. {17} You say, 'I am rich; I have acquired wealth and
do not need a thing.' But you do not realize that you are wretched,
pitiful, poor, blind and naked. {18} I counsel you to buy from me
gold refined in the fire, so you can become rich; and white clothes to
wear, so you can cover your shameful nakedness; and salve to put
on your eyes, so you can see.

{19} Those whom I love I rebuke and discipline. So be earnest, and
repent. {20} Here I am! I stand at the door and knock. If anyone
hears my voice and opens the door, I will come in and eat with him,
and he with me.

{21} To him who overcomes, I will give the right to sit with me on
my throne, just as I overcame and sat down with my Father on his
throne. {22} He who has an ear, let him hear what the Spirit says to
the churches."

This is the last of the seven notes to the seven churches contained within the one letter we call the book of Revelation. To each of these notes I have given a key word which summarizes the key issue facing the churches. The key words also represent key qualities that every Christian should possess in his or her character. Let us refresh our memory of the previous six key words. Ephesus: "love"; Smyrna: "faithfulness"; Pergamum: "holiness"; Thyatira: "truth"; Sardis: "watchfulness"; Philadelphia: "kingportunity."

The key word for Laodicea is "zeal." Their problem is reasonably well known among Christians today. Many pastors might have preached on the church at Laodicea. Their disease is lukewarmness, and the cure is zealousness. It is not only a cure but also a preventative. The greatest prevention for complacency is zeal. One who is truly zealous for the Kingdom would have little time to be complacent. We need to be mindful, however, that the disease of complacency develops over a long period of time; it does not occur overnight. It spreads particularly in an environment of wealth, comfort and prosperity, where there is an absence of persecution or trials.

The church at Laodicea is the last church in every sense of the word. Its letter is the last in the list of seven. It also has the worst ranking, as it is the only church that did not receive any commendation from Christ. Every other church had something positive said about it, but not this one.

The Laodicean Disease

In verse 15, Jesus pronounced: *"I know your deeds, that you are neither cold nor hot. I wish you were either one or the other!"* This church was diagnosed as having contracted the deadly disease of lukewarmness. This pronouncement was absolutely correct and indisputable. It was delivered by the one who is *"the Amen, the faithful and true witness and the ruler of all creation."* The verdict of the Creator supersedes whatever the creature may think of itself.

It is worth noting, in verse 15, that the Laodicean's deeds reflected their lukewarmness. Jesus knew their deeds. He had measured them. They revealed a distinct lack of zeal. Their Christian life and service revealed a desperate lack of commitment and enthusiasm. I wonder if our service for the Lord reflects a lack of enthusiasm. Is our commitment to Him mediocre at best?

The Laodicean church needed to hear the warning of Jesus in verse 16: *"So, because you are lukewarm — neither hot nor cold — I am about to spit you out of my mouth."* Understanding their historical context would help here. The city of Laodicea had a major water supply problem. They had had to build a six-mile-long aqueduct to supply the city with water, which was lukewarm. Jesus said Laodicea was neither cold (like the cold, pure water of Colossae) nor hot (like the therapeutic hot springs of Hierapolis). The lukewarm water which arrived at the city served as an appropriate illustration for a tasteless, good-for-nothing Christianity.

Spiritually speaking, it would have been better for the church to be either cold or hot. If they were cold, asleep or dead, Jesus would command them to wake up or be resurrected. They probably wouldn't argue, since dead men don't put up a fight. They were in a situation that was worse than the cold of death. They were partially and pretentiously active. They were comfortable in their lukewarmness. They had a false sense of security that prevented a cure. They were experiencing the "frog in the pot" syndrome.

The Cure

Fortunately, though their situation was desperate, it wasn't hopeless. The Faithful One initiated a counseling session with them. They needed to do three things if they wanted to be cured of their disease.

First, they needed to acknowledge the predicament they were in. In 3:17 Jesus said, *"You say, 'I am rich; I have acquired wealth and do not need a thing.' But you do not realize that you are wretched, pitiful, poor, blind and naked."* They were to stop denying their true state of affairs. Denial was part of their problem. It would seem reasonable to assume that the church had been engaging in a debate with the Holy Spirit. It would be fair to say that the Spirit had been wanting to help them see the truth of their pitiful state for some time. I cannot help but feel that they were arguing back.

When Jesus speaks to us through the Spirit, we must not argue with Him. We will not win. We will only experience His gentle but sometimes painful discipline. What we hear and don't heed, we will prove in our experience. For instance, if the Spirit says I've got a temper problem, and I don't believe it, I will prove it in my experience. A situation could well arise in which I lose my temper. Then the Spirit will do His work of conviction.

The Laodiceans were saying to themselves, *"I am rich; I have acquired wealth and do not need a thing"* (verse 17). They were behaving just like the culture of their city. Laodicea earned its wealth in the textile industry with the production of black wool and in the banking industry. It was their wealth that built the six-mile-long stone pipe to solve the water problem. The Laodicean claim to be rich and prosperous is reflected in the self-reliant refusal of this city to accept Roman aid for rebuilding after an earthquake in about A.D. 60.

The real problem of the Laodicean Christians was not their material wealth but their self-sufficiency and faulty spiritual perception. They thought they had no need and convinced themselves they were doing well. They needed reality therapy. They had to come out of their denial and acknowledge their sin of self-sufficiency. As long as they refused to acknowledge their wretched and pitiful position, there would be no genuine repentance and no hope for a cure.

Admitting our wrong and our sin takes courage. Counselors know all too well that unless their clients acknowledge their own problems and take responsibility for their own actions, they will not be healed. Often a husband who goes to marriage counseling attacking his wife will need to also acknowledge his own contribution to the problem. A helpless gambler who does not acknowledge his addiction will not even seek help. The same is true for those afflicted with the disease of complacency.

Second, they needed to receive healing from Jesus. They needed to follow the specific counsel of Jesus in verse 18: *"I counsel you to buy from me gold refined in the fire, so you can become rich; and white clothes to wear, so you can cover your shameful nakedness; and salve to put on your eyes, so you can see."* They were invited by Christ to buy genuine gold, that which has been refined in the fire. To me, this speaks of godliness of character, which is produced through the Refiner's fire. This discipline is out of Christ's love for them (verse 19). It is the kind of gold that their wealth cannot buy. It reflects the spiritual poverty of the Laodicean Christians.

They were also asked to buy from Jesus white clothes, befitting a spiritual prince. They were naked and indecently exposed, like the vain king in "The Emperor's New Clothes." This is also in contrast to the black wool for which Laodicea was famous. Clothes of righteousness can only be received from Christ.

The final item they were to purchase from their ultimate Healer was ointment for the healing of vision. Laodicea was famous for its medical school which formulated an ointment for the treatment of ears and an eye salve. But for their spiritual blindness they needed the healing of Jesus in order to see their true condition. The basic thrust of the third part of verse 18 is that they were to go to Jesus and receive humbly what they truly needed.

Third, they needed to be zealous. *"So be earnest, and repent,"* Jesus commanded in verse 19. The Greek word for *"earnest"* here is the word for *zeal.* It is also an imperative in the present continuous tense, which means it is a command to be obeyed now, tomorrow and always. We are to keep being zealous, and not rely on the zeal of yesteryear. The Greek is also a highly charged word that is not devoid of emotion. To be zealous means to have strong affection toward something or be ardently devoted to someone. It means to be jealous or fervent. It is an intense and passionate word. In the NIV it is translated as "jealous," "envy" and "covet" in different places.

The object of our zeal is crucial here. Zeal does not occur in a vacuum. One has to be earnest about something or someone. Many Ozzies are zealous about footie (football – Australian Rules). As Christians, we are to be zealous for Christ Himself and for His Kingdom. We are to be ardent in our devotion to Jesus. We are to be earnest for spiritual gifts, to *"eagerly desire"* them (1 Corinthians 14:1, same Greek word). We are to be earnest for the purposes of the Kingdom of God, the fulfillment of the Great Commission.

How does one become zealous for Christ? First, we must decide to be zealous. It is our choice, our decision. We are to choose to obey Christ's command to be earnest. We need to decide once and for all that we will pursue Him. Second, we need to heed verse 20, to experience intimate fellowship with Him. To the Christians at Laodicea, Jesus said, *"Here I am! I stand at the door and knock. If anyone hears my voice and opens the door, I will come in and eat with him, and he with me."* Look at the initiatives Jesus took toward the Laodicean church. He wrote to them, assured them of His faithfulness, rebuked them out of love, counseled them in wisdom, and reached out to them in verse 20. Zeal is rejuvenated and maintained through intimate fellowship with Jesus. We are not able to work up zeal within ourselves, not for long anyway. Only the Holy Spirit can produce zeal in us, and that happens when we fellowship with Him. The word of God, prayer and worship are crucial elements in this process.

One other way to maintain our zeal is to know and pursue our callings. God has given each of us spiritual gifts that we are to use for His Kingdom. Using our gifts and pursuing our ministry callings help to keep the fire of the Spirit burning. Paul urged Timothy to fan into flame the gift of God that was in him (see 2 Timothy 1:6).

The Promise and the Challenge

All seven letters end with a note of promise. Essentially, it is the promise of eternally reigning with Christ. For the Laodicean Christians, it will be having the right to sit with Christ on His throne. As in all previous letters, they needed to be overcomers. For each of these churches, there are things that need overcoming. They are able to be overcomers in all things, because Christ has overcome the world.

On each occasion, the Spirit had spoken. Each time the exhortation was given: *"He who has an ear, let him hear what the Spirit says to the churches."* Each church was to heed what the Spirit said to it specifically and what was said to other churches as well. I wonder what might the Spirit be saying to you today. Is it something to do with first love, or faithfulness in spite of difficulty? Is it something to do with truth and holiness? Perhaps it is watchfulness and Kingdom opportunity that you need to attend to. Or you may need to be zealous and repent of your complacency. Whichever the case, my prayer is that you will be an overcomer so that you may share in the promise of His eternal Kingdom.

Questions for Private Study and Discussion

1. What, do you think, is the Laodicean disease, and how does one contract it?

2. When the Spirit speaks, we need to obey and not argue. What we hear and don't heed, we'll prove in our experience. What does this mean, and do you agree? Have you experienced this truth?

3. What is the cure for the Laodicean disease?

4. How can we practically maintain our Christian zeal?

5. What is the role of the Spirit in producing and maintaining zeal?

Chapter 10

I AM ON THE THRONE

Revelation 4:1-11:

After this I looked, and there before me was a door standing open in heaven. And the voice I had first heard speaking to me like a trumpet said, "Come up here, and I will show you what must take place after this." {2} At once I was in the Spirit, and there before me was a throne in heaven with someone sitting on it. {3} And the one who sat there had the appearance of jasper and carnelian. A rainbow, resembling an emerald, encircled the throne. {4} Surrounding the throne were twenty-four other thrones, and seated on them were twenty-four elders. They were dressed in white and had crowns of gold on their heads. {5} From the throne came flashes of lightning, rumblings and peals of thunder. Before the throne, seven lamps were blazing. These are the seven spirits of God. {6} Also before the throne there was what looked like a sea of glass, clear as crystal.

In the center, around the throne, were four living creatures, and they were covered with eyes, in front and in back. {7} The first living creature was like a lion, the second was like an ox, the third had a face like a man, the fourth was like a flying eagle. {8} Each of the four living creatures had six wings and was covered with eyes all around, even under his wings. Day and night they never stop saying:

"Holy, holy, holy is the Lord God Almighty, who was, and is, and is to come."

{9} Whenever the living creatures give glory, honor and thanks to him who sits on the throne and who lives for ever and ever, {10} the twenty-four elders fall down before him who sits on the throne, and worship him who lives for ever and ever. They lay their crowns before the throne and say:

{11} *"You are worthy, our Lord and God, to receive glory and honor and power, for you created all things, and by your will they were created and have their being."*

It took seven chapters to get through chapters 2 and 3 of Revelation, but things will pick up speed from now on. Revelation 4 gives us a vivid picture of an unseen reality. But it is a reality no less than the air we breathe. We are not able to see or touch the oxygen we need, but we all know how vital and real it is. Similarly, Heaven is the unseen reality we often miss. In fact, the rest of the book of Revelation deals much with this unseen realm of spiritual reality. It also presents to us a dramatic picture of how Heaven interacts with earth. The spiritual realm affects the physical realm much more than we normally think.

Revelation 4 marks the beginning of a new scene. Verse 1 begins with *"After this I looked ... ."* This is like the movie camera shifting to shoot the start of another scene. It is also worth remembering that John was beholding a real vision. It was not just his imagination. He was not just having a dream. He was actually seeing a vision.

"After this I looked, and there before me was a door standing open in heaven. And the voice I had first heard speaking to me like a trumpet said, 'Come up here, and I will show you what must take place after this.' " It is not good exegesis to read the Rapture of the Church into this verse. The voice of Jesus was declaring to John the purpose of the vision. It was to show John what must take place in the future. The reason is so that the saints will be prepared for what is to come. The intention of Jesus was not to satisfy curiosity. Notice that it says *"must"* take place. What is spoken of here will definitely happen. It occurs in the future, but we can see shadows of it throughout history and in our own times. We are not to be utterly surprised by the future, no matter how awesome or ugly. The purpose of Revelation is to equip us for that reality so that when it comes we will be able to stand firm in the faith.

The Throne

"At once I was in the Spirit, and there before me was a throne in heaven with someone sitting on it" (verse 2). What was the first thing John saw

in Heaven? It was the throne. The throne is the primary focus of this chapter. It is mentioned ten times here. Note that the throne was not empty. Someone was sitting on it. God the Father, the Ancient of Days, was on the throne.

The fact that God was on His throne speaks of God being in charge, governing the universe. It speaks of His sovereignty, His providence and the execution of His divine will. Nothing is left to chance. History is not a random occurrence of uncontrollable events. Evil will not be left unpunished. Justice will be done eventually, in the fullness of time. There is an answer to suffering. There is meaning in life. Are you glad that in the midst of the chaos and confusion we often see in our world, God is on the throne? I am glad that the throne is not empty! I am glad that it is God who is on the throne, and not some mere mortal. God is not surprised by anything that happens on the earth. He does not fall off his chair when some catastrophe occurs, such as earthquakes, wars or genocide. Similarly, God is not surprised by any difficulties or tragedies that may happen in our lives. Further, He has provided a way through for us in every situation. I am glad He is sovereignly governing with power and mercy on His throne.

One of the things that impresses me about this vision of the future is that it begins with God. This may not be our natural expectation. If someone of reliable reputation declared, "I have seen a vision of the future for the earth and mankind," what would be your expectation of that future? Would it focus on Armageddon? the end of the world? the fate of Lucifer? angelic battles? the fate of the earth?

If there was ever a movie depicting the future of the human race, it is "Star Trek." Whether it be the original series with Captain Kirk and Spock or "The Next Generation" with Captain Picard and Data, the *Enterprise* "boldly goes where no one has gone before." The focus is on our ability to unite and explore the universe. The future is ours to create; it begins with the human race. That is a common and natural response when it comes to imagining our future. It begins and ends with us.

Revelation 4 shows us the right perspective regarding our future. It begins with God on His throne. This is the correct perspective of futurology. This is the biblical perspective. One of the hardest lessons for us to learn as human beings is that we are not the center of the universe.

Science has shown us that earth is not the center of the universe. It is not even the center of our solar system. The sun does not circle the earth as people thought for centuries. Similarly, mankind is not the center of the universe. God is. Consequently, God's Kingdom is more important than our history or our future. Furthermore, we are not the center of the Church. Christ is, and so is His Kingdom. This perspective has far-reaching implications for how we live our lives and how we view our circumstances.

Think about it. How often do we get angry at God because things don't go our way? When God does not grant us our wish in our way according to our timing, we might be disappointed and even depressed. This is a common and understandable reaction. But why do we react that way? Could it be because we succumb to thinking that we are the center of the universe? I am not talking about selfishness here. I am referring to a general human predisposition to see ourselves as the center of things. Take another example. When something bad happens to us, are we not tempted to ask "Why me?" with the assumption that it ought not to happen to us? Sure, it is all right to inquire as to why God has allowed things to happen in order to determine an appropriate response. But we need to be careful that this does not reflect a "human-centered" universe rather than a "throne-room" perspective. I am not saying that we are not allowed to feel sad or disappointed at all about pain and suffering, but we do need to evaluate our thinking and perspective to make sure they are in line with Scripture.

Now on to verse 3, where it describes the One on the throne. How on earth does anyone describe God? *"And the one who sat there had the appearance of jasper and carnelian. A rainbow, resembling an emerald, encircled the throne."* What is the appearance of jasper? Jasper is often a highly colored, crystalline quartz substance. Revelation 21:11 refers to its brilliance. What about carnelian? It is a type of red quartz. Thus putting the appearance of jasper and carnelian together, we get a picture of colorful brilliance. It produced a rainbow effect encircling the throne. John was beholding an incredibly colorful and brilliant vision of God on His throne. There are limits to this description in that John could only use human language alluding to substances found on earth. John was not even describing the face of God, just the aura emanating from the Almighty.

The Twenty-four Elders

"Surrounding the throne were twenty-four other thrones, and seated on them were twenty-four elders. They were dressed in white and had crowns of gold on their heads" (verse 4). Who were these twenty-four elders? Some contend that they represent the people of God, with twelve from the Old Testament and twelve from the New. The twelve from the New Covenant would have to be the apostles. While this scenario is possible, I consider it unlikely for two reasons. First, John could not recognize any of them. If one of the "apostolic elders" was Peter or James, John would have recognized him. He might have been tempted to think, *Where is my spot?* ! Second, in Revelation the elders seem to be differentiated from the Christians (see 5:9,10 and 14:3). They may not be humans at all. It seems probable that they were exalted spiritual beings of a unique order.

In the end, who they were is not important to the thrust of the chapter. What is important is what they did before the throne of God. Verses 10 and 11 tell us that they fall down to worship God and take off their golden crowns. Their golden crowns would have been a gift of honor given to them by the Almighty, yet they were to lay them down in worship. This is the proper and acceptable response in the worship of God. If the twenty-four elders as exalted beings would respond to the presence of God that way, how much more we ordinary human beings? When we worship God, we too are to lay down our crowns — our achievements and possessions — so that we may appropriately declare His Lordship over all. Worship is an act of surrender and submission. It is an expression of our love, devotion and dependence on God. Is that our attitude when we participate in worship services at church?

The Living Creatures

"Also before the throne there was what looked like a sea of glass, clear as crystal. In the center, around the throne, were four living creatures, and they were covered with eyes, in front and in back" (verse 6). What these creatures actually represent no one knows. There are at least twenty-two interpretations concerning them. Some say they represent creation, which I doubt. Others say they are the same seraphs as in Isaiah 6, but these

have six wings. Once again, what they represent is not crucial for the chapter as much as their function. *"Day and night they never stop saying: 'Holy, holy, holy is the Lord God Almighty, who was, and is, and is to come'"* (verse 8). One of their primary functions is the worship of God. They are like worship leaders.

The four living creatures and the twenty-four elders have a similar function. They declare to all creation the supremacy of the throne of God. Their confession is that even these exalted creations of God owe their existence to God. They declare the holiness and might of God, that He is the great I AM — who was and is and is to come. God is the only One worthy of worship, because He is the Creator and Sustainer of all things. If God were to withdraw His sustaining power, the universe would immediately cease to function. The world would collapse. The sun would not shine, and the earth would stop spinning. All life on earth would cease to exist!

We cannot add to the glory of God or the honor of God by our worship. We can only declare it as we should. Why? Because all that is good in the universe emanates from Him. Not only is God the Sustainer of all creation, He is the Sustainer of all goodness and love, laughter and joy.

Implications

What practical implications does this chapter have for us who live on the earth? There are four:

First, for those seven churches who were hearing this for the first time, Jesus wanted to assure them as to who is in ultimate control before revealing to them the turbulent future. As they can face their future, we can face ours. God is on His throne. Remember, nothing is going to happen tomorrow that He and you together cannot handle.

Second, because He is the sovereign King, His promises are trustworthy. What He promises, He performs. Isaiah 14:27 says, *"For the LORD Almighty has purposed, and who can thwart him? His hand is stretched out, and who can turn it back?"* Isaiah 46:11 reads, *"I have spoken, and I will bring it to pass; I have planned, and I will do it"* (NRSV). A close friend once gave me a card when I was going through a very difficult time. It read: "What He promises, He performs."

I AM on the Throne

Third, because He is on the throne, prayer is powerful. Some of God's will is executed only in answer to our prayers. This is the way He has designed the coming of His Kingdom, in response to the prayers of the saints. Biblically, all Christians are "saints." The sovereignty of God does not negate the necessity of prayer, but rather highlights it. God's sovereignty does not make our cooperation useless; it guarantees our effectiveness. Your prayers, regardless of how you might feel, are powerful.

Fourth, because God is on the throne, we His people can be victorious in all circumstances. Truly the gates of Hell shall not prevail against those who contend for the Kingdom. When Jesus spoke about the gates of Hell not prevailing against us in Matthew 16:18, He was not referring to our defense but offense. When I was a young Christian, I had this image of Christians huddling together being protected by God against the advance of the enemy. But that is not what Jesus was meaning. Rather, it is the people of God advancing into enemy territory and the gates of Hell can do absolutely nothing to stop us.

I am glad God is on His throne!

Questions for Private Study and Discussion

1. Why does Jesus reveal to us the future?

2. What does it mean for this vision of the future to begin with God on His throne?

3. What practical implications does the "human-centered" perspective of the universe have for Christians?

4. Why is it important for us to "lay down our crowns" when we worship God?

5. Explain the practical implications of God being on His throne.

Chapter 11

THE RISEN LAMB

Revelation 5:1-14:

Then I saw in the right hand of him who sat on the throne a scroll with writing on both sides and sealed with seven seals. {2} And I saw a mighty angel proclaiming in a loud voice, "Who is worthy to break the seals and open the scroll?" {3} But no one in heaven or on earth or under the earth could open the scroll or even look inside it. {4} I wept and wept because no one was found who was worthy to open the scroll or look inside. {5} Then one of the elders said to me, "Do not weep! See, the Lion of the tribe of Judah, the Root of David, has triumphed. He is able to open the scroll and its seven seals."

{6} Then I saw a Lamb, looking as if it had been slain, standing in the center of the throne, encircled by the four living creatures and the elders. He had seven horns and seven eyes, which are the seven spirits of God sent out into all the earth. {7} He came and took the scroll from the right hand of him who sat on the throne. {8} And when he had taken it, the four living creatures and the twenty-four elders fell down before the Lamb. Each one had a harp and they were holding golden bowls full of incense, which are the prayers of the saints. {9} And they sang a new song:

"You are worthy to take the scroll and to open its seals, because you were slain, and with your blood you purchased men for God from every tribe and language and people and nation. {10} You have made them to be a kingdom and priests to serve our God, and they will reign on the earth."

{11} Then I looked and heard the voice of many angels, numbering thousands upon thousands, and ten thousand times ten thousand. They encircled the throne and the living creatures and the elders. {12} In a loud voice they sang:

Risen Lamb, Empowered Saints

"Worthy is the Lamb, who was slain, to receive power and wealth and wisdom and strength and honor and glory and praise!"
{13} Then I heard every creature in heaven and on earth and under the earth and on the sea, and all that is in them, singing:
"To him who sits on the throne and to the Lamb be praise and honor and glory and power, for ever and ever!"
{14} The four living creatures said, "Amen," and the elders fell down and worshiped.

There is enough theology in this chapter worthy of a year's meditation. Profound theological truths such as the helplessness of man and our incapacity to save ourselves, the plan of God in the Gospel, and the Great Commission are all contained in this chapter. The central focus is the Lamb of God that was slain, now risen in mighty power. There is enough truth in this chapter to be worth a lifetime's appropriation or reception, and savoring. It is sufficient both to feed the mind and to nurture the heart.

This chapter is a continuation of the vision John saw in chapter 4. Previously, John saw the Creator, God the Father, on the throne, both ruling and sustaining the universe. It is through Him that all things exist and have their being. Now John sees the Redeemer, who is also on the throne. He is none other than Jesus Christ, the Lamb of God.

None Was Worthy

The first thing that John sees in chapter 5 is a scroll: *"Then I saw in the right hand of him who sat on the throne a scroll with writing on both sides and sealed with seven seals"* (verse 1). This is an unusual scroll, because ancient scrolls normally had writing on one side but not both. That this had writing on both sides indicates the extensiveness and comprehensiveness of the message. One of the longest ancient Egyptian scrolls was found to be 133 feet long.

Without a doubt, this is a very important scroll. It was held in the right hand of God, clearly symbolizing its significance. The seal was a sign of protection and authentication for scrolls. That this was sealed with God's seal represents its divine authenticity. It was sealed with seven seals, indicating that it represents the will of God for the earth and its inhabitants. Most ancient scrolls were sealed with just one seal, except for wills, which were sealed with seven seals. This also symbolizes that it is the complete will of God that *"must take place."* The scroll is God's will for the future. It involves world affairs and concerns the destiny of humankind. Our destiny, and that of our children and grandchildren, is contained in the scroll.

"And I saw a mighty angel proclaiming in a loud voice, 'Who is worthy to break the seals and open the scroll?' " (verse 2). The scroll could not be opened by just anyone. It had to be opened by one who is worthy. The answer to the angel's question was *"No one."* *"But no one in heaven or on earth or under the earth could open the scroll or even look inside it"* (verse 3). No one in all of Heaven or earth could open it and read its content. Not even the angels, neither Michael, nor Gabriel, could perform the act. If none of the angels nor the twenty-four elders could break the seals, we can be sure that it was also true for those who live on the earth. The deafening answer was that no one was worthy! As a result, John wept bitterly (verse 4).

The scroll had to be opened for the will of God to be executed. It had to be opened if there was to be divine justice. For the vindication of the saints (Christians) who were persecuted, and for their prayers to have meaning, the scroll had to be opened. The seals would have to be broken for the sovereignty of God to have effect. The scroll had to be unlocked and read because your future and mine rests in it.

It is absolutely essential that the scroll be opened, but it cannot be done by anyone. Why? Are not the angels worthy enough? Even they are not sufficiently worthy because whoever opens it is also responsible for the execution of it. That is what opening the scroll implies. It is not like a book or a letter that anyone can open and read. Worthiness to open the scroll here means the ability to carry out its will. It is not information but enforcement. It is not passive observation regarding God's will for the future but active intervention to bring it about. As one commentator puts it, the angel's call in verse 2 is for someone "worthy to perform the supreme service of bringing history to its foreordained consummation."

If the scroll could not be opened, it meant that God's will would not be accomplished. Many questions would remain unanswered. Therefore, John wept uncontrollably. At this point he felt the depth of hopelessness for himself, for his churches and for humankind. Issues like the problem of evil, suffering and Satan all would have to be dealt with through the opening of that scroll. If they were not, the meaning of existence would be unresolved: Why are we here? Where are we going? What is the point of it all?

Think of how much those in the church at Smyrna would be on the edge of their seats as they listened to this letter being read. What would be the meaning of their persecution and martyrdom if the scroll could not be opened? Their suffering would have been for nothing. In our case in the twenty-first century, it would be pointless being a Christian or even going to church if the scroll remained sealed.

One needs to experience the gravity of the situation here in verses 1 to 4 before we move on. Unless we appreciate the depravity of our human condition, we will not appreciate the profoundness of God's solution. Nothing and no one can save us — not our cleverness, not our technology or inventions, not our pitiful limited knowledge of science and human nature. All is vanity, and meaningless. That was why John wept uncontrollably. Let us also weep with him.

But There Is One Who Is Worthy

"Then one of the elders said to me, 'Do not weep! See, the Lion of the tribe of Judah, the Root of David, has triumphed. He is able to open the scroll and its seven seals' " (verse 5). Thankfully, there is One who is worthy to open the scroll and execute its contents. This is why the rest in Heaven were not weeping. They were beholding the solution before their eyes. It was *"the Lion of the tribe of Judah, the Root of David."* He is worthy.

This title, "the Lion of the tribe of Judah," occurs only once in the entire Bible, which is here in Revelation 5. It is symbolic of power and strength, as lions are usually depicted as such in the Old Testament. The Lion of the tribe of Judah has triumphed in might. He is the powerful deliverer, the Messiah. He is the One worthy to break the seals and open the scroll.

At this point, John's mood would have changed. He would have caught on to the excitement of the angels and the twenty-four elders. They were beholding the mighty Lion of Judah. John was told not to weep, but to turn and see for himself.

The Lion Is the Lamb

When John looked around expecting to see the mighty and triumphant Lion of Judah, he was utterly surprised because he saw a Lamb. This would have been strange, because John was told to behold the Lion. A lamb is probably the exact opposite of a lion. Lions eat lambs. A lamb is a weak and defenseless animal. How can the Lamb be strong enough to break the seals? Is the Lion of the tribe of Judah really the Lamb of God?

Furthermore, it was a Lamb that looked *"as if it had been slain"* (verse 6). What can be weaker than a lamb but one that was slain? The picture here is one of an animal that had been butchered. It would have been a very graphic vision John saw — a Lamb that was slain. The Lion turned out to be the Lamb!

But the Lamb was not dead. Instead, it was alive and standing upright. A closer look revealed that it was no ordinary lamb. It had seven horns and seven eyes. Horns were symbolic of strength in the Old Testament. This one had seven, symbolizing perfect strength. It was powerful and mighty, after all. Furthermore, the Lamb had seven eyes, *"which are the seven spirits of God sent out into all the earth"* (verse 6). The seven spirits of God are none other than the Holy Spirit, who is the Spirit of Jesus, the Spirit of the Lord. And it is theologically right that the Spirit was poured out only after Jesus' ascension. The Spirit is the representative of Jesus in our midst. The Spirit is now at work on the earth, bringing about the fulfillment of God's will.

This is a great vision of the Trinity. We know from chapter 4 that God the Father was on the throne. Now standing in the center of the throne is the Lamb, Jesus the Messiah. Going forth from the throne is the Holy Spirit, sent out into all the earth.

From this point onward, the Lamb becomes the major focus in the book of Revelation. The Lamb is mentioned twenty-eight times. The title *"the Lion of the tribe of Judah"* is not used again. I believe this is significant. The Lamb is not weak but mighty and to be feared. However, He gained His authority through suffering and death. Christ won the victory through the cross. The Lion and the Lamb are the same, but the biblical focus is on the Lamb. The mighty Lamb that was slain reflects the true understanding of biblical power and strength. It is those who lose their life that will find it. It is through our weakness that the grace and power of God are made perfect. It is through dying to self that we experience the power of the resurrection. This is the nature of the Kingdom, because it is the Kingdom of the Lamb.

The values of the Kingdom reflected in the image of the Lamb are in great contrast to the values of the world. In the world, power is commonly gained by coercion, manipulation or the plain use of brute force, as demonstrated in military regimes. Worldly strength is commonly flaunted externally through wealth or status. The ability to dominate or control others is a sign of power. In the Kingdom of the Lamb, humility and servanthood are the true signs of strength.

Bowls of Incense

In verse 7, the Lamb stepped forward and took the scroll. When He had taken it, *"the four living creatures and the twenty-four elders fell down before the Lamb. Each one had a harp and they were holding golden bowls full of incense, which are the prayers of the saints"* (verse 8). The bowls of incense contained the prayers of the saints. In this context of worship, the bowls were offered up to God. The prayers of Christians have significance now because the Lamb was able to open the scroll. Their prayers can now be answered!

In the world, the prayers of believers are despised as weak and powerless. Prayer is seen by some as a crutch for those who cannot help themselves. It is perceived as a cop-out, outdated and useless for modern technological people. But here in Revelation 5 the significance of the prayers of the saints is captured marvelously. They are contained in golden bowls, offered to God in worship by the twenty-four elders! What is despised in the world is precious in God's sight.

Our prayers are of great value in the Kingdom of the Lamb. The Lamb is known in the world as weak but now it is mighty in Heaven. Similarly, our prayers are seen as useless in the world, but they are powerful in Heaven. This will be more evident in later chapters.

I am often reminded of this when I pray for our church planters in Living Impact thousands of kilometers (or miles) away. I reside in Australia, and they live in different parts of Asia. Sometimes I am tempted to feel that my prayers are pointless. But deep within, I know they are not. They are being collected in golden bowls of incense before the presence of God. And He will answer them!

Mission Possible

The chapter concludes with great worship. They sang a new song that had never been sung before in Heaven. What was the content of that song? Whatever it was it must have been significant given the context in which it was presented. It was dedicated to the risen Lamb upon the throne! If you or I were writing its lyrics, we would sweat for months to perfect it. What would we include in it?

Fortunately, we are told its content in verses 9 and 10. Verse 9 says, *"You are worthy to take the scroll and to open its seals, because you were slain, and with your blood you purchased men for God from every tribe and language and people and nation."* Salvation for all peoples of the earth from every tribe and language is a vital part of this new song. This demonstrates the priority of the Great Commission in Scripture. Now the reason the Lamb was considered worthy to break the seals and open the scroll is stated: *"because you were slain, and with your blood you purchased men for God."* The Lamb is worthy because of His death and resurrection, bringing us salvation. This is the true Gospel of Christ. Also, this Gospel is to be preached to all tribes and peoples of the earth. This is the Great Commission of the Lamb.

In the ministry of Living Impact we are glad to play a small part in this Kingdom purpose. Some have become Christians in the unreached parts of Asia through the ministry of our indigenous church planters. We rejoice with Heaven at this great news. We believe with all our hearts that more will be added to the Kingdom of the Lamb as the Gospel spreads to places it has never been. Many living there have never heard the Gospel even once!

In this new song of chapter 5 we have Christology and missiology integrated. None of us should be in any doubt about the centrality of the Lamb in the Gospel — both the death and the resurrection of Christ. We should also be fully convinced of the significance of the Great Commission. This Gospel is to be preached to every tribe and people on the earth. The Lamb was slain for them! Fulfilling the Great Commission is the one eternally significant thing we can do on earth that we cannot do when we get to Heaven.

All the angels then sang in a loud voice to God the Creator and the Redeemer: *"Worthy is the Lamb, who was slain, to receive power and wealth and wisdom and strength and honor and glory and praise! To him who sits on the throne and to the Lamb be praise and honor and glory and power, for ever and ever! Amen"* (verse 12).

Questions for Private Study and Discussion

1. Why is it important that someone was found worthy to open the scroll?

2. What are the theological and practical implications of the Lion being the Lamb?

3. What Christian behaviors reflect the values of the Lamb? What is your concept of power?

4. How does the world's view of prayer compare to that of Revelation 5?

5. How does the new song in verses 9 to 14 capture the core of Christology and missiology?

6. In what ways are you participating in the spread of the gospel to the ends of the earth? If possible, check out www.livingimpact. org to investigate how you can participate meaningfully in world missions in the twenty-first century.

Chapter 12

HISTORY UNFOLDING: THE SEALS OPENED

Revelation 6:1-17:

> *I watched as the Lamb opened the first of the seven seals. Then I heard one of the four living creatures say in a voice like thunder, "Come!" {2} I looked, and there before me was a white horse! Its rider held a bow, and he was given a crown, and he rode out as a conqueror bent on conquest.*
>
> *{3} When the Lamb opened the second seal, I heard the second living creature say, "Come!" {4} Then another horse came out, a fiery red one. Its rider was given power to take peace from the earth and to make men slay each other. To him was given a large sword.*
>
> *{5} When the Lamb opened the third seal, I heard the third living creature say, "Come!" I looked, and there before me was a black horse! Its rider was holding a pair of scales in his hand. {6} Then I heard what sounded like a voice among the four living creatures, saying, "A quart of wheat for a day's wages, and three quarts of barley for a day's wages, and do not damage the oil and the wine!"*
>
> *{7} When the Lamb opened the fourth seal, I heard the voice of the fourth living creature say, "Come!" {8} I looked, and there before me was a pale horse! Its rider was named Death, and Hades was following close behind him. They were given power over a fourth of the earth to kill by sword, famine and plague, and by the wild beasts of the earth.*
>
> *{9} When he opened the fifth seal, I saw under the altar the souls of those who had been slain because of the word of God and the testimony they had maintained. {10} They called out in a loud voice, "How long, Sovereign Lord, holy and true, until you judge the inhabitants*

of the earth and avenge our blood?" {11} Then each of them was given a white robe, and they were told to wait a little longer, until the number of their fellow servants and brothers who were to be killed as they had been was completed.

{12} I watched as he opened the sixth seal. There was a great earthquake. The sun turned black like sackcloth made of goat hair, the whole moon turned blood red, {13} and the stars in the sky fell to earth, as late figs drop from a fig tree when shaken by a strong wind. {14} The sky receded like a scroll, rolling up, and every mountain and island was removed from its place.

{15} Then the kings of the earth, the princes, the generals, the rich, the mighty, and every slave and every free man hid in caves and among the rocks of the mountains. {16} They called to the mountains and the rocks, "Fall on us and hide us from the face of him who sits on the throne and from the wrath of the Lamb! {17} For the great day of their wrath has come, and who can stand?"

The stage is set for the future to be revealed. In Revelation 4 we saw God the Father sitting on His throne governing the universe as the Creator. In Revelation 5 we saw that the Lamb of God was worthy to take the scroll and break its seven seals. God's will for the earth and those who live on it can now be executed. The Lamb is now ready to open the scroll and reveal its content.

It is important to remind ourselves at this point that the book of Revelation is not a theological treatise or an academic thesis. Neither is it a crystal ball for us to gaze into the future. It is essentially a pastoral letter written to edify the people of God. It is divinely given to change our lives.

The message contained in this chapter should quicken the heart of any Christian. It will help us who live in the fast pace of the twenty-first century to interpret the world events happening around us. It will help us to pray scripturally regarding those events. And it will assist us to get our priorities right in our lives. It answers at least partially the profound question raised by that great author, Francis Schaeffer: "How should we then live?"

The First Four Seals

Chapter 6 begins the series of seals. Each is opened in turn by the Lamb of God, Jesus Christ. What do the seals represent and how are they relevant to us? How should we interpret them? Let me begin by saying that the first four seals form a set and should be considered together. They each involve a rider on a horse. Each horse is of a different color, and each rider holds a different "weapon." The thing to note is that they form a pattern and are part of each other. We will initially consider them one at a time, but more importantly, we will pull them together to see what they are really saying to us.

The First Seal:

Verse 2 tells us about the first seal: *"I looked, and there before me was a white horse! Its rider held a bow, and he was given a crown, and he rode out as a conqueror bent on conquest."* Here we have the first seal as the rider of Conquest. His function is to facilitate the activity of conquering on the earth. He was given a crown, which means he will be successful and victorious in his purpose. He held a bow, which is symbolic of military might, consistent with interpretations of the bow in the Old Testament. This rider goes throughout the earth to encourage the destructive activity of nations conquering each other. The white color of the horse here would symbolize not purity, but purging. This rider is NOT Jesus Christ.

The history of mankind is full of conquerors and colonizers. Every time a powerful nation conquers a less powerful one, we know that it is related to the rider of Conquest. Think of Spain and Portugal when they divided the known world into two parts, one belonging to Spain and the other to Portugal. The conquistadors of the 1500s were a merciless, conquering lot. Consider Great Britain when she built the British Empire through the colonizing of other nations such as Hong Kong, Malaya and India. The same spirit of Conquest was at work in Germany and Japan during World War II. The rider of Conquest is still at work today.

Did God cause all this to happen? Are the riders good or evil? These questions will be explored later in this chapter.

The Second Seal:

Revelation 6:4 tells us that the second seal is the rider of Strife: *"Then another horse came out, a fiery red one. Its rider was given power to take peace from the earth and to make men slay each other. To him was given a large sword."* He was given power to take peace from the earth. This rider stands for internal strife and ethnic divisions, even within conquering countries. His function is to create tension, hostility, hatred and violence by removing peace from the world.

Once again, it is not difficult to see this throughout history and in our world today. For example, the question of land for a Palestinian state has never been resolved, and it may never be. Yugoslavia went through its ethnic cleansing some years ago. The Hutus and the Tutsies have been wanting to exterminate each other. Fijian Indians and indigenous Fijians can't get along. On a milder scale, we have seen violent protests against the World Economic Forum held in different parts of the world. Subgroups within societies oppose each other — sometimes violently.

One insight that comes out of these seals is the unseen spiritual reality behind the daily activities of men, which has a dynamic effect upon all inhabitants of the earth. Yes, we are responsible for our own actions, but there is another dimension to be reckoned with. True reality is an interaction between the two. This is a significant aspect of spiritual warfare.

The Third Seal:

The third seal is the rider of Scarcity in Revelation 6:5-6: *"When the Lamb opened the third seal, I heard the third living creature say, 'Come!' I looked, and there before me was a black horse! Its rider was holding a pair of scales in his hand. Then I heard what sounded like a voice among the four living creatures, saying, 'A quart of wheat for a day's wages, and three quarts of barley for a day's wages, and do not damage the oil and the wine!' "* What is the meaning of the announcement: *"a quart of wheat for a day's wages"*? A quart of wheat was the equivalent of a day's meal. In other words, all the wage one earns in a day is only sufficient for the purchase of food for that day. It is like a Big Mac costing a day's salary. Imagine someone paying $100 for a Quarter Pounder meal! The key word here is Scarcity, caused by economic havoc such as rampant inflation.

Although the world may not have seen this kind of inflation, some countries have experienced economic chaos. The annual inflation rate in Burma (Myanmar) is officially thirty percent. In the 1990s, we have seen Russians stand in line for hours to buy a loaf of bread. Some coal miners in Russia were not paid for months.

Interestingly, the second part of verse 6 says, *"Do not damage the oil and the wine."* Oil and wine are symbolic of joy and gladness in the Old Testament, and the same might be applied here. If so, it means that there will still be joy in the midst of economic chaos. However, it is also feasible to take oil and wine here as symbolic of wealth, meaning that the scarcity will not be global or all-pervasive. Consequently, there will be a greater divide between the rich and the poor.

The Fourth Seal:

The fourth seal is the rider of Death: *"I looked, and there before me was a pale horse! Its rider was named Death, and Hades was following close behind him. They were given power over a fourth of the earth to kill by sword, famine and plague, and by the wild beasts of the earth"* (verse 8). This rider represents death by famine, war, natural disasters, diseases, plagues and any other form of desolation. Worth noting is that the Grim Reaper is only allowed to take the lives of a quarter of the population. His destruction is limited. As Leon Morris put it: "Even Hades is limited in power by God."

The First Four Seals Considered Together

As mentioned earlier, these four seals should be considered as a set. Five points are worth noting regarding them:

First, the four seals do not represent a single catastrophic event. It is not as though in a particular month or year the world will experience the destruction of the riders all at once. History tells us that Conquest, Strife, Scarcity and Death have been with us for a long time.

Second, the seals are not consecutive events. It is not that one follows after the other, or that one doesn't begin until the other ends. For instance, it is not that the second seal of Scarcity does not begin until the first seal of Conquest concludes. Rather, the four seals occur simultaneously. Their destruction happens concurrently. Even though the seals are opened one after another, the riders are going forth together. They are still riding throughout the earth today. This interpretation is consistent with historical reality. Conquest, Strife, Scarcity and Death have been occurring simultaneously in history.

Third, the seals increase in intensity as history moves to its conclusion. Although destruction and desolation have been with us even before the book of Revelation was written, these forces become more prevalent as we approach the Second Coming of Christ. For instance, even though people were dying from wars before the birth of Jesus, almost ten million died in World War I, and fifty-five million died in World War II. Since 1900, about one million have died from earthquakes.

Fourth, these seals are not caused by God. In all four seals the word *"given"* is used. The riders are given permission to do what they were restrained from doing. It is like the book of Job, where Satan was given permission to test Job. Yet with each rider there is a limit as to the extent of the destruction that he can cause. Therefore, these riders are not angels, but evil forces under the sovereign restraint of God's almighty power. Conquest, Strife, Scarcity and Death are not caused by God, but they are permitted to occur on the earth as the reality of spiritual warfare takes place.

Fifth, these tragic events do not represent God's direct hand of judgment on mankind. They are different from the seven "bowls" of wrath which occur later in Revelation. God's judgment will come later. As we shall see, its effects will be far worse.

Perhaps we might ask: "Why does God not stop all this evil? Is He all-powerful or not? If He is, why does He allow this suffering? When will God intervene?" These are legitimate questions which we will now consider.

The Fifth Seal

The fifth seal concerns the souls of martyrs: *"When he opened the fifth seal, I saw under the altar the souls of those who had been slain because of the word of God and the testimony they had maintained"* (verse 9). These believers were persecuted and killed for the faith. Their souls were now in Heaven.

"They called out in a loud voice, 'How long, Sovereign Lord, holy and true, until you judge the inhabitants of the earth and avenge our blood?' " (verse 10). They were essentially asking the same question we raised earlier: "Why does God not do anything and when will He act?" They were crying out for vindication, not for personal revenge. "How long?" they queried. Notice that they asked with reverence and respect, knowing that God is the *"Sovereign Lord, holy and true."*

The reason for the seeming delay is given in the next verse: *"Then each of them was given a white robe, and they were told to wait a little longer, until the number of their fellow servants and brothers who were to be killed as they had been was completed"* (verse 11). The number of martyrs has to be fulfilled before the end will come. We must not see this as sadistic, as though God has a set target for how many Christians He wants killed before He will do anything. The implication here is the spread of the Gospel. The Gospel needs to be proclaimed to the ends of the earth to every tribe and language and people. The cost will be martyrdom for many, of whom the number only God has the knowledge. Just as there is a set number of martyrs to be fulfilled, there is a set number of people who will become Christians. Both must be completed for the end to come. Once again, we see the importance of the Great Commission.

This gives us a clue as to how to pray when confronted with the trage-dies represented by the first four seals. Regardless of any conquest, strife, scarcity and death, the Gospel needs to go forward. People need to be saved through the Gospel of the Lamb. We need to pray that the Gospel will give hope, especially to those who are suffering from war, famine and poverty. In countries where there is persecution, we need to pray that even more will come to know the Lamb of God as their Savior and Lord. Is that not the greatest reward for martyrs, that many more come to the faith as a result of their deaths? We can remind ourselves that it was during the decades of persecution in Communist China that the house churches grew like wildfire.

The Sixth Seal

Now we come to the sixth seal of cosmic catastrophe. This seal is awesome, horrific and terrible: *"I watched as he opened the sixth seal.*

There was a great earthquake. The sun turned black like sackcloth made of goat hair, the whole moon turned blood red, and the stars in the sky fell to earth, as late figs drop from a fig tree when shaken by a strong wind. The sky receded like a scroll, rolling up, and every mountain and island was removed from its place" (verses 12-14). It is a shocking depiction of the end of the world as we have it. If taken literally, it sounds almost like a description of the earth being impacted by a giant meteor. According to experts, if ever a one-mile-wide asteroid were to hit the earth, it would create a massive earthquake, we would not be able to see the sun because of a global dust storm, the sky would appear to roll back, and gigantic waves would hit our shores, covering our cities in water. I am not saying that this is what is being described here in verses 12 to 14. But it pays to note that even a literal interpretation is not unfathomable.

We need to ask ourselves where else in the New Testament do we read about this description. It is in Matthew 24, Mark 13 and Luke 21, all descriptions of the end of the age by Jesus Himself. The parallel between these passages and the entire sixth chapter of Revelation is profound. It should not surprise us that Jesus had spoken of this while He was on earth. It is He who was revealing the future to John in Revelation.

The following table reveals the parallel between Matthew 24:6-29 and Revelation 6. In Matthew 24, Jesus was speaking of the end of days to His disciples.

Here's a table highlighting the parallel between Revelation 6 and Matthew 24:

Revelation 6	Matthew 24
Seal 1: Conquest	Verse 6: Wars
Seal 2: Strife	Verse 7: Ethnic division
Seal 3: Scarcity	Verse 7: Famine and earthquakes
Seal 4: Death	

"The end is still to come."   (Matthew 24:6)
"All these are the beginning of birth pains."   (Matthew 24:8)

Seal 5: Martyrs	Verse 9: Persecution and martyrdom
	Verse 14: Gospel preached to all Ethnic groups
Seal 6: Cosmic catastrophe	Verse 29: Cosmic disaster

Whether Revelation 6:12-14 is a literal description of the end, or a figurative depiction or some combination, it presents a frightening scenario. Every man, woman and child will be fearstruck: *"Then the kings of the earth, the princes, the generals, the rich, the mighty, and every slave and every free man hid in caves and among the rocks of the mountains"* (verse 15). The sixth seal is nothing less than the final judgment of God. The next two verses make this clear: *"They called to the mountains and the rocks, 'Fall on us and hide us from the face of him who sits on the throne and from the wrath of the Lamb! For the great day of their wrath has come, and who can stand?'"* The Lamb of God is indeed mighty and to be feared. As Mounce put it: "Nothing short of the awesome dissolution of the world itself will strike terror to the heart of man in the last days."

That day will be a fearful and frightful day for two groups of people in particular. The first will be those who have consistently heard the Gospel but have repeatedly rejected its message. The second will be those who have a relationship with the Lamb but have persistently abused it. They are like those in the Laodicean church who have shut Christ out of their hearts even though they are saved.

Those who are committed to following Him should rejoice on that great Day of the Lamb. Like the wise ones in the parable of the virgins, they have kept their oil burning and are ready for the Second Coming. God wants all of us to be in this group. The choice is always ours.

According to Jesus in Luke 21:34, all of us need to be careful in the last days: *"Be careful, or your hearts will be weighed down with dissipation, drunkenness and the anxieties of life, and that day will close on you unexpectedly like a trap."* The "anxieties of life" can weigh us down, even to the extent of making us unprepared.

The everyday life can bog us down, says Jesus in Matthew 24:37-39: *"As it was in the days of Noah, so it will be at the coming of the Son of Man. For in the days before the flood, people were eating and drinking, marrying and giving in marriage, up to the day Noah entered the ark; and they knew nothing about what would happen until the flood came and took them all away. That is how it will be at the coming of the Son of Man."* This was spoken in the context of the end of the world. We know there is nothing scripturally wrong with getting married, as marriage is God ordained. But we can get so caught up with ordinary living that we become unprepared for the Day of the Lamb. Let us always remember the importance of the Gospel and the significance of the Great Commission.

Now that was the sixth seal. What about the seventh? If the sixth was the end of the world, what else is there? And what about the question asked in Revelation 6:17, *"For the great day of their wrath has come, and who can stand?"* The next several chapters will address these questions.

Questions for Private Study and Discussion

1. Why are the four seals unlikely to be a single catastrophic event or consecutive catastrophic events?

2. How would the first four seals help us to interpret history and world events?

3. What implications does the fifth seal have for our prayers?

4. How can we prepare ourselves for the Day of the Lamb?

5. How can we avoid being bogged down spiritually by the events of everyday life?

Chapter 13

EMPOWERED SAINTS:
THE SEALING OF THE 144,000

Revelation 7:1-17:

After this I saw four angels standing at the four corners of the earth, holding back the four winds of the earth to prevent any wind from blowing on the land or on the sea or on any tree. {2} Then I saw another angel coming up from the east, having the seal of the living God. He called out in a loud voice to the four angels who had been given power to harm the land and the sea: {3} "Do not harm the land or the sea or the trees until we put a seal on the foreheads of the servants of our God." {4} Then I heard the number of those who were sealed: 144,000 from all the tribes of Israel.

{5} From the tribe of Judah 12,000 were sealed, from the tribe of Reuben 12,000, from the tribe of Gad 12,000, {6} from the tribe of Asher 12,000, from the tribe of Naphtali 12,000, from the tribe of Manasseh 12,000, {7} from the tribe of Simeon 12,000, from the tribe of Levi 12,000, from the tribe of Issachar 12,000, {8} from the tribe of Zebulun 12,000, from the tribe of Joseph 12,000, from the tribe of Benjamin 12,000.

{9} After this I looked and there before me was a great multitude that no one could count, from every nation, tribe, people and language, standing before the throne and in front of the Lamb. They were wearing white robes and were holding palm branches in their hands. {10} And they cried out in a loud voice:

"Salvation belongs to our God, who sits on the throne, and to the Lamb."

{11} All the angels were standing around the throne and around the elders and the four living creatures. They fell down on their faces before the throne and worshiped God, {12} saying:

"Amen! Praise and glory and wisdom and thanks and honor and power and strength be to our God for ever and ever. Amen!"

{13} Then one of the elders asked me, "These in white robes — who are they, and where did they come from?"

{14} I answered, "Sir, you know."

And he said, "These are they who have come out of the great tribulation; they have washed their robes and made them white in the blood of the Lamb. {15} Therefore, "they are before the throne of God and serve him day and night in his temple; and he who sits on the throne will spread his tent over them. {16} Never again will they hunger; never again will they thirst. The sun will not beat upon them, nor any scorching heat. {17} For the Lamb at the center of the throne will be their shepherd; he will lead them to springs of living water. And God will wipe away every tear from their eyes."

This chapter represents an important interlude between the seals in chapter 6 and the trumpets in chapters 8 and 9. Here in chapter 7 the answer to the question raised at the conclusion of the previous chapter is answered. The question in Revelation 6:17 was: *"For the great day of their wrath has come, and who can stand?"* Indeed, who could stand before the wrath of God? Well, there is a group of people who could stand righteous before the Lamb, and here we will see who they are. We could ask ourselves, "Are we part of that group?"

The chapter begins with four angels standing at the four corners of the earth, holding back the four winds (verse 1). This verse has nothing to do with cosmology, as some have contended. For instance, it is not making a statement about whether the earth is flat. Two points are worth noting here. First, the four angels are not the four riders considered in chapter 6. The four riders are not angels, whereas these are. These four are good angels holding back the four winds. Second, the four winds are winds of destruction, which fits the nature of the first four trumpets in the next chapter. The winds are not only the destructive forces of nature; they also represent political forces. That they include political forces is shown in Daniel 7:2-3, *"Daniel said: 'In my vision at night I looked, and there before me were the four winds of heaven churning up the great sea. Four great beasts, each different from the others, came up out of the sea.' "* It is clear in Daniel that the beasts represented political empires. Thus, the winds in Revelation 7:1 represent natural and political forces of destruction, held back by the angels until the 144,000 are sealed.

The Sealing of the 144,000

"What is the sealing of the 144,000? What does it mean to be sealed? How does it happen?" These may be some of the questions people ask. "Does each one literally get a stamp on their foreheads, representing their sealing?" Perhaps not.

There are not many occasions when the New Testament talks about sealing the people of God. However, the times when it does are revealing for our purpose. Let us note some of these verses:

2 Corinthians 1:21-22: *"Now it is God who makes both us and you stand firm in Christ. He anointed us, set his seal of ownership on us, and put his Spirit in our hearts as a deposit, guaranteeing what is to come."*

Ephesians 1:13: *"And you also were included in Christ when you heard the word of truth, the gospel of your salvation. Having believed, you were marked in him with a seal, the promised Holy Spirit,"*

Ephesians 4:30: *"And do not grieve the Holy Spirit of God, with whom you were sealed for the day of redemption."*

In these three verses, the focus is on the Holy Spirit. The Spirit is our seal, a sign of God's ownership, guaranteeing what is to come. Therefore, the sealing of the 144,000 will have something to do with the Holy Spirit. Keep that in mind.

An important verse worth noting at this point is Revelation 14:1: *"Then I looked, and there before me was the Lamb, standing on Mount Zion, and with him 144,000 who had his name and his Father's name written on their foreheads."* Though this verse does not explicitly refer to the sealing of the 144,000, it is relevant in that the forehead is symbolic of the character and lifestyle of a person. This means the 144,000 possess a character and lifestyle matching that of the Lamb. This speaks to me clearly of the fruit of the Spirit, evident in the life of believers.

Pulling all these verses together, we begin to see a picture of what the sealing of the 144,000 is referring to. Sealing in the New Testament refers to the Holy Spirit dwelling in Christians. In the context of Revelation 7, it refers to a special protection that comes from the Holy Spirit, shielding from the wrath of God to come. It is similar to the final plague experienced by Egypt but not by the Israelites in Moses' day. The 144,000 will be protected from the destruction of the fifth and sixth trumpets, which will be considered in the next two chapters. All this emphasizes to us the importance of the Holy Spirit in our lives, especially as we draw closer to the end of the age. Every believer has the Holy Spirit dwelling in him or her. We need to make sure we are daily walking in the Spirit, and that we are empowered by Him.

The Identity of the 144,000

Who are these 144,000 who are sealed? Are we included? Do they represent Christians throughout history, or are they just Christian Jews? Are they a select group, like the Jehovah's Witnesses?

Before I enter into discussion regarding the identity of this elite group, let me say something about the number 144,000 itself. The number is not literal. Remember that Revelation contains many symbolic numbers. Furthermore, 144,000 seems too complete to be taken literally in the context of chapter 7: twelve thousand from twelve tribes. Indeed, it is most likely a number which symbolizes completeness. Consider this: 144 = 12 x 12, and 1000 = 10x10x10. Both 12 and 10 are biblical numbers representing completeness. John was saying that everyone who was to be included is included — none were missing. All who were supposed to be protected by the Spirit will be protected. There will be no omission by the Almighty One. The Shepherd knows His sheep. No one can snatch us out of His hands.

Now let us consider some possibilities regarding their identity. First, some have argued that these represent the Old Testament people of God. In other words, Israel. The listing of the twelve tribes is cited as evidence for this interpretation. However, it should be noted that by John's time, ten of the twelve tribes have already disappeared in the Assyrian invasion of Israel. What would be the point of sealing them if they are already dead? Furthermore, Revelation as a book focuses on the New Covenant community of God, not on the Old Covenant people. Note too that the list of tribes begins with Judah and not Reuben. And Dan was omitted, while Manasseh was inserted.

Second, others have contended that while they may not be Old Testament Jews, they are Christian Jews. Once again, the citing of the twelve tribes in verse 5 to 8 is used as supporting evidence. However, the greatest argument against this interpretation is that Revelation focuses away from the natural Jewish heritage. It was mentioned twice in the seven letters that the true Jew is not one by ancestry but one who is a Christian. Furthermore, most of the original hearers of Revelation were not Jews, but Gentile Christians. In addition, the focus of the New Testament itself is that the people of God under the New Covenant are neither Jews nor Greeks, but ones who are born again in Christ. Therefore, it makes little biblical sense to interpret the 144,000 as referring only to Jewish Christians.

Third, some have said they represent martyrs coming out of the Great Tribulation. This interpretation seems more plausible than the previous two. However, the context of chapter 7 emphasizes not just martyrs, but Christians. The focus is on those who are saved by the Lamb, martyred or not.

The most likely interpretation is that these 144,000 represent all Christians who will go through the Great Tribulation, regardless of whether they are Jews or Gentiles, martyrs or not. They are sealed with the unique protection of the Holy Spirit, kept from the onslaught of demonic forces unleashed in the fifth and sixth trumpets. Ironically, many will be martyred.

The Great Multitude and the Great Tribulation

What is the identity of the great multitude? Are they the 144,000? What is the Great Tribulation, and when will it happen?

Let us attempt to step into John's shoes up to verse 9, where it says: *"After this I looked and there before me was a great multitude that no one could count."* In verse 4, John heard the number of those who were sealed: 144,000. Now, in verse 9, he looked to see who they were. Wouldn't you want to see who these were? He looked, and what did he see? He saw the great multitude. The 144,000 who were sealed were the great multitude. They were uncountable, because the number was not a literal one: *"a great multitude that no one could count."* Importantly, they were *"from every nation, tribe, people and language."* They were not just Christian Jews, but also Gentiles!

"Then one of the elders asked me, 'These in white robes — who are they, and where did they come from?' I answered, 'Sir, you know.' And he said, 'These are they who have come out of the great tribulation; they have washed their robes and made them white in the blood of the Lamb' " (verses 13-14). It is clearly indicated here that the 144,000 are those who came out of the great tribulation. In other words, they do not represent all the people of God throughout history. Neither do they represent all Christians throughout Church history. They are specifically those who go through the Great Tribulation.

What is the Great Tribulation, and when will it happen? Let me first give a suggestion as to what it is not. The Great Tribulation is not equivalent to "the last days" in the biblical meaning of the term. Scripturally, "the last days" began on the Day of Pentecost. Peter quoted from Joel in his Pentecost sermon and referred to this day as the beginning of "the last days." This is not the Great Tribulation referred to here.

The phrase *"great tribulation"* in the original language only occurs on four occasions in the New Testament. Twice it refers to the end. In Matthew 24, the phrase is translated *"great distress"* (NIV): *"For then there will be GREAT DISTRESS, unequaled from the beginning of the world until now — and never to be equaled again. If those days had not been cut short, no one would survive, but for the sake of the elect those days will be shortened"* (Matthew 24:21-22). This is most probably not referring to the time from Pentecost onward, but rather to the very end. In the context of Revelation 7, it refers to the time before the blowing of the trumpets.

This is not to minimize the times of testing and tribulation Christians and martyrs have experienced throughout Church history. There were, no doubt, seasons of severe tribulation encountered by believers, especially in the twentieth century. However, the final wave of tribulation is a gigantic tsunami. That is the Great Tribulation. Importantly, we should note that it will be a Great Tribulation for all mankind, not just for Christians.

Questions for Private Study and Discussion

1. How does "sealing" relate to the Holy Spirit?

2. What are the arguments against interpreting the 144,000 to be only Jewish Christians?

3. What are the arguments for interpreting the 144,000 to be all believers who will go through the Great Tribulation?

4. How does the Bible understand "the last days"?

5. What is the Great Tribulation?

6. If you are to go through the Great Tribulation, what is the best protection you can have as a Christian? How does it relate to the power and fruit of the Spirit?

Chapter 14

THE EARTH CHANGES: THE CALL TO AWAKEN
(Revelation 8 and 9)

Revelation 8:

When he opened the seventh seal, there was silence in heaven for about half an hour.

{2} And I saw the seven angels who stand before God, and to them were given seven trumpets.

{3} Another angel, who had a golden censer, came and stood at the altar. He was given much incense to offer, with the prayers of all the saints, on the golden altar before the throne. {4} The smoke of the incense, together with the prayers of the saints, went up before God from the angel's hand. {5} Then the angel took the censer, filled it with fire from the altar, and hurled it on the earth; and there came peals of thunder, rumblings, flashes of lightning and an earthquake.

{6} Then the seven angels who had the seven trumpets prepared to sound them.

{7} The first angel sounded his trumpet, and there came hail and fire mixed with blood, and it was hurled down upon the earth. A third of the earth was burned up, a third of the trees were burned up, and all the green grass was burned up.

{8} The second angel sounded his trumpet, and something like a huge mountain, all ablaze, was thrown into the sea. A third of the sea turned into blood, {9} a third of the living creatures in the sea died, and a third of the ships were destroyed.

{10} The third angel sounded his trumpet, and a great star, blazing like a torch, fell from the sky on a third of the rivers and on the springs of water — {11} the name of the star is Wormwood. A third

of the waters turned bitter, and many people died from the waters that had become bitter.

{12} The fourth angel sounded his trumpet, and a third of the sun was struck, a third of the moon, and a third of the stars, so that a third of them turned dark. A third of the day was without light, and also a third of the night.

{13} As I watched, I heard an eagle that was flying in midair call out in a loud voice: "Woe! Woe! Woe to the inhabitants of the earth, because of the trumpet blasts about to be sounded by the other three angels!"

From now on we will be tackling two chapters of Revelation at a time. The stage is set for the trumpets to be blown. In the last chapter we saw the sealing of the 144,000, those who will go through the Great Tribulation. The interlude of chapter 7 is passed, and chapter 8 is the beginning of scene three.

These two chapters we are about to consider are very relevant to our high-tech postmodern society. We have entered the twenty-first century. The season for the unfolding of these terrible events described is so much closer. We can almost feel it in the air, so to speak. The Day of the Lord is indeed drawing extremely near. The question we need to ask ourselves again is: "How should we then live? What constitutes the urgency of this season?" In contrast to the teachings of some, Christians will go through these events like everyone else. Therefore, we need to be ready, equipped and prepared, as there will not be any Rapture of the Church before the Second Coming of Jesus.

The Prayers of the Saints

Chapter 8 begins with Jesus opening the seventh seal. Remember that only six seals have been opened up to this point. In chapter 6 we saw the opening of the first six seals, but not the seventh seal. Now the time has come for the final seal, with its seven trumpets, to be revealed.

"When he opened the seventh seal, there was silence in heaven for about half an hour. And I saw the seven angels who stand before God, and to them were given seven trumpets" (verses 1-2). The seventh seal contains a series

of seven trumpets, ready to be blown by seven angels. This series of trumpets is introduced by half an hour of silence, which highlights the significance of these trumpets. John must now be at the edge of his seat. The silence would have been awe-inspiring. It is the only time in the entire book of Revelation that we have silence in Heaven. Up till now the angels, ten thousand times ten thousand of them, the twenty-four elders and the multitude were all praising the God of Heaven who sits upon the throne. The four living creatures have never ceased to pronounce, *"Holy, holy, holy, is the Lord God Almighty."* Now, there is silence!

It seems that it was during this half hour of silence that verses 2 to 4 took place. Seven angels were handed seven trumpets. One angel stood before the altar with a golden censor full of incense, which are the prayers of Christians. It might have been like watching a silent movie. The silence was broken in verse 5: *"Then the angel took the censer, filled it with fire from the altar, and hurled it on the earth; and there came peals of thunder, rumblings, flashes of lightning and an earthquake."* The prayers of Christians, which have been collected in the golden fire pan, are now hurled toward the earth in answer to their prayers. God will begin to avenge the martyrs, who have been asking: *"How long, Sovereign Lord, holy and true, until you judge the inhabitants of the earth and avenge our blood?"* (6:10).

In these first five verses of chapter 8, the main focus is on God's response to the prayers of Christians. The answer to their prayers lies in the blowing of the seven trumpets. This demonstrates to us the importance of our prayers in relation to the unfolding of world history. What would have happened if Christians had not prayed or had given up half-way? The golden bowls (see Revelation 5:8) would not have been filled. God's response would have been delayed.

This is a lesson for us that sometimes our prayers seem to go unanswered. But God is storing them up for the proper time. We are not to give up praying regardless of how discouraging circumstances may be — lest the golden bowl not be filled with the incense of intercession. Psalm 141:2 says, *"May my prayer be set before you like incense; may the lifting up of my hands be like the evening sacrifice."* When the time is right, God will answer.

It is also worth noting that some prayers may not be answered in our lifetimes. Many martyrs in John's day and since have prayed for deliverance but have died at the hand of their persecutors. Are their prayers not answered? Is God's hand too short to save? Of course not. Their prayers will be answered eventually, but beyond their lifetimes. There will be judgment and vindication at the end — every deed of man is accounted for. It's a solemn reminder of the reality that the grand plan of God does not have to fit within our limited physical lifespans. The Kingdom of God is greater than we are.

The First Four Trumpets

The trumpets are about to be blown by the angels. What is their

Seals 1-5

Conquest
Scarcity
Strife
Death
Martyrdom

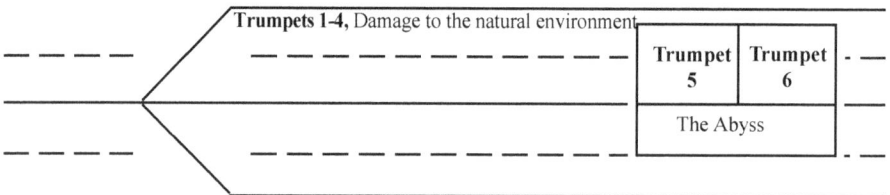

Trumpets 1-4, Damage to the natural environment

Trumpet 5 Trumpet 6

The Abyss

Seal 6
The Wrath of God

content? What do they mean? How do they relate to the six seals that have already been opened? Importantly, if the sixth seal was to be the end, the climax, and the conclusion, what do we make of the trumpets that are to follow? As the diagram above illustrates, the seventh seal (which reveals the seven trumpets) is the expansion of the sixth seal. It tells us in greater detail the content of the sixth seal. It expands and enlarges for us the events which occur at the very end.

The Earth Changes: The Call to Awaken

We will consider the first four trumpets together since, like the first four seals in chapter 6, they go together as a set. Three comments are worth noting concerning them in general. First, trumpets are used here because the context picks up three important functions of trumpets in the Old Testament. They were used for introducing important announcements, for the waging of war, and for the calling of soldiers to get ready for battle. All these aspects are relevant to our context here in chapter 8. The trumpets announce the coming of the wrath of God in the outpouring of the bowls later on. They also sound the call for the final battle and for Christians to get ready for the Great Tribulation. The second general point I wish to make is that the first four trumpets occur simultaneously, and not consecutively. Like the four riders of the first four seals, they occur at the same time. Third, the first four trumpets are not single catastrophic events. They happen over a set duration. This differs from the fifth and sixth trumpets, as we shall see.

In the first trumpet, *"A third of the earth was burned up, a third of the trees were burned up, and all the green grass was burned up"* (verse 7). The description of *"hail and fire mixed with blood"* (verse 6) does not need to be taken literally. The important thing is to consider its effects. There was significant damage to the earth's vegetation and greenery. In other words, agriculture was greatly affected by this trumpet. However, only a third of the earth was damaged, meaning that the destruction was significant but partial.

In the second trumpet, *"A third of the sea turned into blood, a third of the living creatures in the sea died, and a third of the ships were destroyed"* (verse 9). Once again, the description of what caused it, *"something like a huge mountain, all ablaze, was thrown into the sea"* (verse 8), need not be interpreted literally. What is significant is the effect of marine life being destroyed, with its consequences for the fishing industry.

The third trumpet resulted in the poisoning of the rivers and springs: *"A third of the waters turned bitter, and many people died from the waters that had become bitter "*(verse 10). The picture of a falling star by the name of "Wormwood" is figurative. It is unlikely to be a meteor. The meaning of *Wormwood* in Hebrew is "bitterness," and it is used seven times in the Old Testament (e.g. Proverbs 5:4, NRSV). In the Greek it means "undrinkable." Once more, it is the result of the trumpet that is the focus. In this case, it represents the polluting and poisoning of our waters. It is a fact even now that a significant amount of the earth's water is undrinkable, and there is in the twenty-first century a great clean water shortage in parts of Asia and Africa.

In the fourth trumpet, the sun, moon and stars are struck, resulting in partial darkness across the earth: *"A third of the day was without light, and also a third of the night"* (verse 12). This trumpet represents significant damage to the earth's atmosphere.

What do we see when we pull all four trumpets together? We see the partial but significant destruction of our natural environment as never before. The earth is greatly damaged. The important thing to note here is the consequences of this damage for human beings. Our vegetation, marine life, water supply and atmosphere are all adversely affected. The interesting thing about this is that we can read about environmental damage almost daily in newspapers, magazines and books.

Does this mean that the four trumpets are describing the environmental havoc we hear about today? I am not sure. However, what we see now might be but a prelude to what is coming. Incredibly, fifty years ago it would have been difficult to imagine the effects of these trumpets. Now, it is not so difficult. We have been hearing about global warming, water pollution, food shortages and other environmental degradation for some years now. Remember, these trumpets are not single catastrophic events but events that occur over time. I believe we are witnessing the prelude to these trumpets.

Perhaps we might ask: "How can the environmental damage of the earth be God's judgment? Isn't it our own fault?" The answer to both questions is yes. The trumpets represent God's passive judgment by allowing for the winds of destruction to blow upon the earth (see Revelation 7:1-3). It is possible and within the testimony of Scripture for God to judge us simply by withholding His mercy and allowing us to have our own way. Up to now, it has been God who stopped us from totally destroying ourselves.

Christians, though sealed with the protection of the Spirit, will not escape the consequences of the first four trumpets. They will, however, be miraculously protected from the effects of the next two.

The Earth Changes: The Call to Awaken

Revelation 9:

The fifth angel sounded his trumpet, and I saw a star that had fallen from the sky to the earth. The star was given the key to the shaft of the Abyss. {2} When he opened the Abyss, smoke rose from it like the smoke from a gigantic furnace. The sun and sky were darkened by the smoke from the Abyss. {3} And out of the smoke locusts came down upon the earth and were given power like that of scorpions of the earth. {4} They were told not to harm the grass of the earth or any plant or tree, but only those people who did not have the seal of God on their foreheads. {5} They were not given power to kill them, but only to torture them for five months. And the agony they suffered was like that of the sting of a scorpion when it strikes a man. {6} During those days men will seek death, but will not find it; they will long to die, but death will elude them.

{7} The locusts looked like horses prepared for battle. On their heads they wore something like crowns of gold, and their faces resembled human faces. {8} Their hair was like women's hair, and their teeth were like lions' teeth. {9} They had breastplates like breastplates of iron, and the sound of their wings was like the thundering of many horses and chariots rushing into battle. {10} They had tails and stings like scorpions, and in their tails they had power to torment people for five months. {11} They had as king over them the angel of the Abyss, whose name in Hebrew is Abaddon, and in Greek, Apollyon.

{12} The first woe is past; two other woes are yet to come.

{13} The sixth angel sounded his trumpet, and I heard a voice coming from the horns of the golden altar that is before God. {14} It said to the sixth angel who had the trumpet, "Release the four angels who are bound at the great river Euphrates." {15} And the four angels who had been kept ready for this very hour and day and month and year were released to kill a third of mankind. {16} The number of the mounted troops was two hundred million. I heard their number.

{17} The horses and riders I saw in my vision looked like this: Their breastplates were fiery red, dark blue, and yellow as sulfur. The heads of the horses resembled the heads of lions, and out of their

mouths came fire, smoke and sulfur. {18} A third of mankind was killed by the three plagues of fire, smoke and sulfur that came out of their mouths. {19} The power of the horses was in their mouths and in their tails; for their tails were like snakes, having heads with which they inflict injury.

{20} The rest of mankind that were not killed by these plagues still did not repent of the work of their hands; they did not stop worshiping demons, and idols of gold, silver, bronze, stone and wood — idols that cannot see or hear or walk. {21} Nor did they repent of their murders, their magic arts, their sexual immorality or their thefts.

The Fifth Trumpet

If we think that the first four trumpets are terrible, the fifth and sixth trumpets are worse. They happen consecutively, one after another. The final three trumpets are also called woes because of their severity upon mankind. The fifth trumpet describes the army of locusts rising from the Abyss: *"The fifth angel sounded his trumpet, and I saw a star that had fallen from the sky to the earth. The star was given the key to the shaft of the Abyss. When he opened the Abyss, smoke rose from it like the smoke from a gigantic furnace. The sun and sky were darkened by the smoke from the Abyss. And out of the smoke locusts came down upon the earth and were given power like that of scorpions of the earth"* (verses 1-3). The star is Satan, who fell from Heaven, and was given the key to the Abyss. *Abyss* means "depthless" in the Greek and equates with "the bottomless pit." It is the abode of demonic spirits (cf. Luke 8:31).

That Christians will be protected from the harm of this trumpet is seen in verse 4: *"They were told not to harm the grass of the earth or any plant or tree, but only those people who did not have the seal of God on their foreheads."* The locusts were given permission to attack not the environment, but humans who are not sealed with the Spirit. It is clear that this trumpet is still in our future.

A few points are worth noting about these locusts. First, they are not your natural locusts. They possess tails that sting like scorpions. Second, they have teeth like lions' teeth, which bite. Third, they have human faces, symbolic of their intelligence. Fourth, they are organized in a military structure. Finally, and most important, these locusts are not from God. They originate from the Abyss. They are clearly demonic: *"They had as king over them the angel of the Abyss, whose name in Hebrew is Abaddon, and in Greek, Apollyon"* (verse 11). "Abaddon," or "Apollyon," is a destroying principality who receives his orders from Satan.

What is the marching order of these demonic locusts? Their function is to torture human beings, but not kill them: *"They were not given power to kill them, but only to torture them for five months. And the agony they suffered was like that of the sting of a scorpion when it strikes a man"* (verse 5). The pain is so great and unbearable that men would rather die than suffer its torment. *"During those days men will seek death, but will not find it; they will long to die, but death will elude them"* (verse 6). This is ironic, since many Christians will be martyred in those days by mankind, yet the inhabitants of the earth will now long for the death they cannot find.

The Sixth Trumpet

"The first woe is past; two other woes are yet to come. The sixth angel sounded his trumpet, and I heard a voice coming from the horns of the golden altar that is before God. It said to the sixth angel who had the trumpet, 'Release the four angels who are bound at the great river Euphrates.' And the four angels who had been kept ready for this very hour and day and month and year were released to kill a third of mankind" (verses 12-15). The four angels released here are not the same ones as at the beginning of chapter 7. Like Apollyon, they are evil beings in charge of demonic forces of destruction.

What demonic forces are released this time? There are two hundred million of these mounted troops (verse 16). *"The horses and riders I saw in my vision looked like this: Their breastplates were fiery red, dark blue, and yellow as sulfur. The heads of the horses resembled the heads of lions, and out of their mouths came fire, smoke and sulfur"* (verse 17). Their marching order was to kill by three specific plagues: *"A third of mankind was killed by the three plagues of fire, smoke and sulfur that came out of their mouths.*

The power of the horses was in their mouths and in their tails; for their tails were like snakes, having heads with which they inflict injury" (verses 18-19).

It is difficult to know exactly what these plagues refer to. Perhaps it could be a new kind of bacterium or germ more horrific than the ebola virus. It is medically recognized that the world is poised to suffer from a new kind of epidemic that is immune to antibiotics. On the other hand, it could denote some form of biochemical destruction engineered by humans. This is not inconceivable. We do know that these forces of destruction in the sixth trumpet are demonic in nature, and therefore are not your standard viruses or bacteria. Some commentators interpret this trumpet to refer to cancer and traffic accidents. This seems highly unlikely, since cancer and traffic accidents affect Christians and non-Christians alike. It is difficult to argue that cancer is demonically driven, from the details given here. They are describing extremely unusual times that have not yet occurred on the earth.

Remember, the fifth and sixth trumpets do not affect those who are sealed with the Spirit's protection. How might this happen? It would have to be a miracle indeed. It will happen similarly to what occurred with the plagues in Egypt. The people of God were protected from the angel of death in the final plague because of the blood of the lamb. Here, those being protected are not Jews, but rather Christians who have been cleansed by the blood of the Lamb and sealed with the Spirit of the Lord.

Conclusion

We need to conclude with verse 20: *"The rest of mankind that were not killed by these plagues still did not repent of the work of their hands."* Repentance is the aim of these trumpets. They sound forth the final wake-up call, the last warning, before the active wrath of God is poured out from the bowls of chapter 16. The verse is also prophetic, that many still will not repent.

The implication for us living in times prior to these trumpets is not to be missed. The season of harvest is now. The time for reaping is now. When the trumpets are eventually blown, very tough times will occur in which few will repent. Hearts will be hardened. But now there is still time, before the commencement of the Great Tribulation. This is why I believe there will be a great harvest of lives for the Kingdom before the trumpets begin. It will be the final great harvest.

Coinciding with the great harvest will be a final great awakening, which will reinforce the global harvest. Christians need to be ready and prepared for what is to come — the commencement of the trumpets. We are already seeing the prelude of it, as the earth changes.

Questions for Private Study and Discussion

1. How does Revelation 8:1-5 address the expectation of wanting all our prayers answered immediately?

2. In what ways does the environmental damage we see today tell us that the beginning of the first four trumpets is near?

3. How do we know that the locusts are demonic?

4. Why is it unlikely that the sixth trumpet refers to events such as the traffic accidents and cancers that we see today?

5. What is the ultimate aim of the fifth and sixth trumpets?

6. In what way is now the time for global harvest and spiritual awakening?

Chapter 15

MIGHTY CHURCH:
THE TWO WITNESSES
(Revelation 10 and 11)

Revelation 10:

Then I saw another mighty angel coming down from heaven. He was robed in a cloud, with a rainbow above his head; his face was like the sun, and his legs were like fiery pillars. {2} He was holding a little scroll, which lay open in his hand. He planted his right foot on the sea and his left foot on the land, {3} and he gave a loud shout like the roar of a lion. When he shouted, the voices of the seven thunders spoke. {4} And when the seven thunders spoke, I was about to write; but I heard a voice from heaven say, "Seal up what the seven thunders have said and do not write it down."
{5} Then the angel I had seen standing on the sea and on the land raised his right hand to heaven. {6} And he swore by him who lives for ever and ever, who created the heavens and all that is in them, the earth and all that is in it, and the sea and all that is in it, and said, "There will be no more delay! {7} But in the days when the seventh angel is about to sound his trumpet, the mystery of God will be accomplished, just as he announced to his servants the prophets."
{8} Then the voice that I had heard from heaven spoke to me once more: "Go, take the scroll that lies open in the hand of the angel who is standing on the sea and on the land."
{9} So I went to the angel and asked him to give me the little scroll. He said to me, "Take it and eat it. It will turn your stomach sour, but in your mouth it will be as sweet as honey." {10} I took the little scroll from the angel's hand and ate it. It tasted as sweet as

honey in my mouth, but when I had eaten it, my stomach turned sour. {11} Then I was told, "You must prophesy again about many peoples, nations, languages and kings."

Revelation 11:

I was given a reed like a measuring rod and was told, "Go and measure the temple of God and the altar, and count the worshipers there. {2} But exclude the outer court; do not measure it, because it has been given to the Gentiles. They will trample on the holy city for 42 months. {3} And I will give power to my two witnesses, and they will prophesy for 1,260 days, clothed in sackcloth." {4} These are the two olive trees and the two lampstands that stand before the Lord of the earth. {5} If anyone tries to harm them, fire comes from their mouths and devours their enemies. This is how anyone who wants to harm them must die. {6} These men have power to shut up the sky so that it will not rain during the time they are prophesying; and they have power to turn the waters into blood and to strike the earth with every kind of plague as often as they want.

{7} Now when they have finished their testimony, the beast that comes up from the Abyss will attack them, and overpower and kill them. {8} Their bodies will lie in the street of the great city, which is figuratively called Sodom and Egypt, where also their Lord was crucified. {9} For three and a half days men from every people, tribe, language and nation will gaze on their bodies and refuse them burial. {10} The inhabitants of the earth will gloat over them and will celebrate by sending each other gifts, because these two prophets had tormented those who live on the earth.

{11} But after the three and a half days a breath of life from God entered them, and they stood on their feet, and terror struck those who saw them. {12} Then they heard a loud voice from heaven saying to them, "Come up here." And they went up to heaven in a cloud, while their enemies looked on.

{13} At that very hour there was a severe earthquake and a tenth of the city collapsed. Seven thousand people were killed in the

earthquake, and the survivors were terrified and gave glory to the God of heaven.

{14} The second woe has passed; the third woe is coming soon.

{15} The seventh angel sounded his trumpet, and there were loud voices in heaven, which said:

"The kingdom of the world has become the kingdom of our Lord and of his Christ, and he will reign for ever and ever."

{16} And the twenty-four elders, who were seated on their thrones before God, fell on their faces and worshiped God, {17} saying:

"We give thanks to you, Lord God Almighty, the One who is and who was, because you have taken your great power and have begun to reign. {18} The nations were angry; and your wrath has come. The time has come for judging the dead, and for rewarding your servants the prophets and your saints and those who reverence your name, both small and great — and for destroying those who destroy the earth."

{19} Then God's temple in heaven was opened, and within his temple was seen the ark of his covenant. And there came flashes of lightning, rumblings, peals of thunder, an earthquake and a great hailstorm.

Chapter 11 of Revelation has been known to be one of the most difficult chapters to interpret in the entire book. It is the one that talks about the two witnesses and the 1,260 days. One commentator has said that the chapter is "extraordinarily difficult to interpret and the most diverse solutions have been proposed." We will surely need the help of the Spirit in order to understand it simply, scripturally and meaningfully. However, we will first tackle the relatively easier chapter 10 before moving to the more difficult chapter 11.

The Mighty Angel

"Then I saw another mighty angel coming down from heaven. He was robed in a cloud, with a rainbow above his head; his face was like the sun, and his legs were like fiery pillars" (10:1). This represents the description of the angel's might. His appearance was awesome both in size and

splendor. His right foot stood upon the sea and his left foot upon the land. He gave a mighty roar like that of a lion. It is interesting that while not all angels are as mighty as this one, we can be certain that angels are not cute, airy-fairy beings that float around with wings. They are ministering spirits capable of waging war with demonic principalities. It is encouraging to remember that we are watched over by these ministering spirits.

When this powerful angel shouted, the seven thunders spoke: *"And when the seven thunders spoke, I was about to write; but I heard a voice from heaven say, 'Seal up what the seven thunders have said and do not write it down' "*(verse 4). This is perhaps unfortunate for us, since if John did not write down what the thunders spoke, we have no way of knowing. What did the thunders say? It must have been important, given the context of the mighty angel's unveiling. But there is no way of knowing, and we must keep our curiosity in check. Nevertheless, it does tell us that not everything is revealed to us in the book of Revelation. We are only told what we absolutely need to know. It also keeps us in suspense.

Another point worth noting here in verse 4 is that John seems to be writing this vision in Revelation as he saw it. This dispels the interpretation of some that John had borrowed from different sources to write the book. Also, it would be highly improbable that he created the story out of his own imagination just to communicate a teaching point. Revelation is scripture inspired by the Holy Spirit. John wrote down for us what he saw.

In verses 6 and 7, the angel gave an oath saying, *"There will be no more delay! But in the days when the seventh angel is about to sound his trumpet, the mystery of God will be accomplished, just as he announced to his servants the prophets."* The time has arrived for God to conclude history. The final woe is about to happen. The last trumpet is about to be blown. The mystery of God will be accomplished and fulfilled — the conclusion of history as we have it. When the final trumpet is blown, the time draws near for the eventual salvation of the people of God. The Second Coming will occur, together with the Rapture of the Church. The wedding supper of the Lamb will take place. Judgment Day will begin. The Gospel will have been preached to the ends of the earth. Every tribe will have heard. The Kingdom of God will fully come. There will be *"no more delay,"* says the angel.

The Little Scroll

Now we come to the most important part of chapter 10: *"Then the voice that I had heard from heaven spoke to me once more: 'Go, take the scroll that lies open in the hand of the angel who is standing on the sea and on the land.' So I went to the angel and asked him to give me the little scroll. He said to me, 'Take it and eat it. It will turn your stomach sour, but in your mouth it will be as sweet as honey.' I took the little scroll from the angel's hand and ate it. It tasted as sweet as honey in my mouth, but when I had eaten it, my stomach turned sour. Then I was told, 'You must prophesy again about many peoples, nations, languages and kings' "* (verses 8-11).

We see here the importance of the little scroll highlighted in two ways. It is in the hands of the mighty angel, which is ironic since the scroll is little but the angel is huge. The message is short but vital. Second, John is commanded to take the scroll and eat it. This means John was to digest the message, as Ezekiel did in Ezekiel 3. The message was both sweet and sour. Why was that? It was sweet because of the eventual victory assured for the saints and the Kingdom of God, but sour because of the suffering and martyrdom of the Church.

Not only was the scroll the Word of God, it was a special word of prophecy relevant to the conclusion of time. It was not just the Gospel, but contained a prophetic word for the end of days. The prophecy has to do with *"many peoples, nations, languages and kings"* about whom John must prophesy (verse 11). The content of the scroll was probably the next four chapters of Revelation (11-14). It is not the entire book of Revelation, which is a long scroll. It is a short message which has to do with the two witnesses, the beasts, world leaders, Christians and the inhabitants of the world. It also has much to do with the Church — how she is to function in such times. John had to prophesy about it, but first he had to understand it. He had to digest the message. And so must we.

The Forty-two Months

We come now to the more difficult chapter eleven whose content is part of the little scroll: *"I was given a reed like a measuring rod and was told, 'Go and measure the temple of God and the altar, and count the worshipers there. But exclude the outer court; do not measure it, because it has been given to the Gentiles. They will trample on the holy city for 42 months'"* (verses 1-2). The main point to note here is the spiritual preservation of the believers, who are the worshipers. The measuring of the temple and the counting of the believers are symbolic of spiritual protection. Christians are preserved from spiritual, not physical, harm during the testing period of the great tribulation. None will be lost. Their names are in the Lamb's Book of Life.

As for the identity of the Gentiles, we need to note that in the context of Revelation, the true Jew is the Christian (cf. 3:9). Remember, this is also the teaching of the rest of the New Testament (see Galatians 1-3). Therefore, the Gentiles are the nonbelievers, the spiritual "non-Jew." Thus, the worshipers that are counted are Christians, but the Gentiles in verse 2 are the non-Christians. These Gentile nonbelievers will *"trample on the holy city for 42 months."*

What is this *"holy city"* referring to in this context? We know that in Revelation 21 the Holy City is the new Jerusalem, and the new Jerusalem is the Church: *"I saw the Holy City, the new Jerusalem, coming down out of heaven from God, prepared as a bride beautifully dressed for her husband"* (21:2). Theologically, we understand the Bride of Christ to be the people of God. Therefore, Gentiles trampling on the holy city means that nonbelievers will severely persecute and martyr Christians. They will physically attack and attempt to destroy the Church. *"They will trample on the holy city for 42 months."*

What is this *"42 months"* being referred to? Is it symbolic or literal? It will be interesting to ask ourselves, "How many days are in 42 months if we assume a thirty-day month?" The answer is 1,260 days, the exact number of days the two witnesses will prophesy: *"And I will give power to my two witnesses, and they will prophesy for 1,260 days, clothed in sackcloth"* (verse 3). In other words, the Church will be severely persecuted for the same period during which the two witnesses will exercise their ministry. These 42 months, or 1,260 days, are also the exact same period which Daniel referred to in Daniel 7:25: *"He will speak against the Most High and oppress his saints and try to change the set times and the laws. The saints will be handed over to him for a time, times and half a time."* Christians will be persecuted by the Antichrist for *"a time, times and half a time,"* which is the equivalent of three and a half years in Daniel's language. Three and a half years is also 42 months or 1,260 days! Importantly, Daniel's phrase *"a time, times and half a time"* was a conventional symbol for a limited duration during which evil reigns. It is not necessarily a literal three and a half years, but can be a symbolic period. This lends weight to interpreting the 42 months, or 1,260 days, as a symbolic short period of time. It is not wrong to take the 42 months as literal, but the above explanation shows it is not necessary to be rigid here.

This period of intense tribulation occurs before the third woe, or the blowing of the seventh trumpet. We know this because of Revelation 11:14: *"The second woe has passed; the third woe is coming soon."* It is during this period that God mightily anoints His two witnesses with extraordinary spiritual power. Who are these witnesses? What is their identity? Are they preachers and teachers, as some have suggested? Are they necessarily two individuals? Are they the return of Moses and Elijah?

The Two Witnesses

Before we consider the identity of *"the two witnesses,"* we shall consider their functions. In Revelation 11:3-12, we see that these two witnesses have four specific functions. First, they testify for Christ. Second, they prophesy for Christ. Third, they perform powerful miraculous signs of judgment. Fourth, they are martyred for Christ.

As for their miracle workings, they have the power of Elijah to call down fire and to withhold rain. They have the power of Moses to generate plagues, although we must be mindful that they are not the same plagues as the sixth trumpet. They are invincible during their time of ministry. They cannot be destroyed until they have fully completed their service at the end of the 1,260 days. After their deaths, for three and a half days, they will be resurrected in great glory (verse 11). *"Then they heard a loud voice from heaven saying to them, 'Come up here.' And they went up to heaven in a cloud, while their enemies looked on. At that very hour there was a severe earthquake and a tenth of the city collapsed. Seven thousand people were killed in the earthquake, and the survivors were terrified and gave glory to the God of heaven"* (verses 12-13).

These functions give a clue as to the possible identity of *"the two witnesses."* A further important clue lies in verse 4: *"These are the two olive trees and the two lampstands that stand before the Lord of the earth."* What are the two olive trees and the two lampstands? The two olive trees and the two lampstands pick up on Zechariah's vision in Zechariah 4. Some years ago I preached a sermon series on Zechariah and Haggai. In Zechariah 4, the two olive trees represented the anointed leadership of Joshua, the high priest, and of Zerubbabel, the governor (verse 8). There was one lampstand in Zechariah 4, which represented the people of God. Oil from the olive branches was flowing into the lamp, symbolic of the Holy Spirit. Indeed, Zechariah 4:6 says, *"This is the word of the LORD to Zerubbabel: 'Not by might nor by power, but by my Spirit,' says the LORD Almighty."* In Zechariah's vision, the leadership and the people were empowered by the Spirit to rebuild the physical Temple. A similar interpretation can be made in Revelation 11.

Taking all our clues together, *"the two witnesses"* most probably represent the anointed leadership and worshippers from the witnessing church. Therefore, *"the two witnesses"* are not necessarily two specific individuals only. The *"witnesses"* are also *"lampstands,"* which are symbolic of churches (cf. Revelation 1:20 and 11:4). That the number *"two"* is mentioned relates to their function of testifying for Christ where a minimum of two witnesses is necessary for a true testimony (cf. Deuteronomy 19:15). Thus, *"the two witnesses"* represent the anointed, witnessing people of God in this period of great tribulation. They are witnessing Christians who are greatly empowered by the Holy Spirit. This does not mean that they cannot also be represented by two individual leaders coming in the power of Moses and Elijah. They might be like John the Baptist, who came in the spirit of Elijah. Therefore, *"the two witnesses"* are the leaders and worshipers of the witnessing church.

Mighty Church: The Two Witnesses

Following the above, there are important implications for the Church now. The effective Church that will witness and prophesy for Christ in the Great Tribulation is the Spirit-empowered Church. It will be a testifying Church as well as a prophesying Church. It will be a miraculous Church where extraordinary signs and wonders are performed. The members will eventually be martyred, as will their anointed leaders. After three days they will be raised from the dead in spectacular fashion before their enemies. This is not the final Rapture of all saints. It is a resurrection of martyred Christians. Not all Christians will participate in this resurrection, as not all will be martyred. Some will remain until the last woe, the final trumpet, has passed.

Questions for Private Study and Discussion

1. The angel said, *"There will be no more delay."* In what ways do you consider this a good thing? In what ways is it not positive?

2. Why might the little scroll be both sweet and sour?

3. What is the significance of the 42 months, both theologically and practically?

4. In what ways are the two witnesses both individuals and churches?

5. What are the functions and characteristics of those witnessing Christians who will go through the Great Tribulation?

6. How can you best prepare yourself for such times?

Chapter 16

CHRISTIANS AND THE BEASTS
(Revelation 12-14)

I hope that as we now enter the second half of Revelation we can see that the book is not impossible to understand. At the same time, we can see that it is very relevant to our lives. Remember that the book was written for the encouragement of the seven churches of Asia Minor in the first century. Here, we see the double-edged application of some Bible prophecies. They have relevance both to the original hearers and to those who come later. The book of Revelation is applicable both to the first-century hearers and to us who read it two thousand years later. For example, chapter 13 discusses the final beast of the Great Tribulation. Yet, in history there have been many shadows of the final beast that have appeared. The apostle John might have considered the Roman Empire to be the beast of chapter 13. The Reformers took the beast to be the Roman Catholic Church of Luther's day. But we who live in the twenty-first century know that the final beast is yet to come. Those that came before were but shadows of the final and most terrible one.

As chapters 12 to 14 tie in together, we will consider them as a block. The main thrust is Satan's persecution of the Church through his two beasts on the earth, and why and how Christians should respond in such times.

The Woman and the Dragon

Revelation 12:

A great and wondrous sign appeared in heaven: a woman clothed with the sun, with the moon under her feet and a crown of twelve stars on her head. {2} She was pregnant and cried out in pain as she was about to give birth. {3} Then another sign appeared in heaven: an enormous red dragon with seven heads and ten horns and seven crowns on his heads. {4} His tail swept a third of the stars out of the sky and flung them to the earth. The dragon stood in front of the woman who was about to give birth, so that he might devour her child the moment it was born. {5} She gave birth to a son, a male child, who will rule all the nations with an iron scepter. And her child was snatched up to God and to his throne. {6} The woman fled into the desert to a place prepared for her by God, where she might be taken care of for 1,260 days.

{7} And there was war in heaven. Michael and his angels fought against the dragon, and the dragon and his angels fought back. {8} But he was not strong enough, and they lost their place in heaven. {9} The great dragon was hurled down — that ancient serpent called the devil, or Satan, who leads the whole world astray. He was hurled to the earth, and his angels with him.

{10} Then I heard a loud voice in heaven say:

"Now have come the salvation and the power and the kingdom of our God, and the authority of his Christ. For the accuser of our brothers, who accuses them before our God day and night, has been hurled down. {11} They overcame him by the blood of the Lamb and by the word of their testimony; they did not love their lives so much as to shrink from death. {12} Therefore rejoice, you heavens and you who dwell in them! But woe to the earth and the sea, because the devil has gone down to you! He is filled with fury, because he knows that his time is short."

{13} When the dragon saw that he had been hurled to the earth, he pursued the woman who had given birth to the male child. {14} The woman was given the two wings of a great eagle, so that she might fly to the place prepared for her in the desert, where she would be taken care of for a time, times and half a time, out of the serpent's reach. {15} Then from his mouth the serpent spewed water like a river, to overtake the woman and sweep her away with the torrent. {16} But the earth helped the *woman by opening its mouth and swallowing the river that the dragon had spewed out of his mouth. {17} Then the dragon was enraged at the woman and went off to make war against the rest of her offspring — those who obey God's commandments and hold to the testimony of Jesus.*

Three key figures are found in chapter 12. They are the woman, her child and the dragon. Who do they represent? What is the significance of this vision? Are there any practical implications? It would make it easier to identify the woman once we have identified the dragon and the child. Let us begin with the easiest of the three: the dragon.

"The great dragon was hurled down — that ancient serpent called the devil, or Satan, who leads the whole world astray. He was hurled to the earth, and his angels with him" (verse 9). There are no prizes for guessing this one, since the answer is plainly stated. The dragon is Satan, the devil. His seven heads and ten horns are symbolic of universal power and complete authority upon the earth. This is true as far as earthly kingdoms are concerned. Paul tells us in Ephesians that he is the prince of the power of the air, and John's gospel declares him to be the prince of this world.

The next figure to identify is the child. Who is this child? The giveaway verse is verse 5: *"She gave birth to a son, a male child, who will rule all the nations with an iron scepter. And her child was snatched up to God and to his throne."* The key phrase is that the child *"will rule all the nations with an iron scepter."* This is a phrase often used of Christ, the Messiah. The dragon wanted to destroy the child at His birth, which we know was what occurred at Jesus' birth. When Jesus finished His ministry, He ascended to Heaven. The child is none other than Jesus Christ, the Son of David.

Now we come to the woman, who gave birth to the child. Before we jump to the conclusion that she represents Mary the mother of Jesus, we need to remember verse 6: *"The woman fled into the desert to a place prepared for her by God, where she might be taken care of for 1,260 days."* Is it likely that this applies to Mary? I think not. More appropriately, the woman represents the one who gave birth to the Messiah. The woman is none other than Israel, the house of David, from which the Son of

David emerged. It was Israel, or Judah, that gave birth to the Messiah, who will sit on the throne of David forever. The woman has a crown of twelve stars, symbolizing, at this point, the twelve tribes of Israel. This was Israel under the Old Covenant, the believing messianic Israelite community, travailing and waiting with agonizing expectation for the birth of the Messiah.

Satan, the dragon, pursued Jesus during His ministry on earth. After the resurrection and ascension, the dragon turns his attention to the woman, who at this point changes her identity to Israel under the New Covenant, the Church. Therefore, the woman represents not so much the new or the old Israel, but the true Israel, the people of God under the Old Covenant before the ascension, and the people of God under the New Covenant after the outpouring of the Holy Spirit. The twelve stars of her crown thus represent both the twelve tribes and the twelve apostles.

"And there was war in heaven. Michael and his angels fought against the dragon, and the dragon and his angels fought back. But he was not strong enough, and they lost their place in heaven. The great dragon was hurled down — that ancient serpent called the devil, or Satan, who leads the whole world astray. He was hurled to the earth, and his angels with him" (verses 7-9). This most likely refers to the battle which took place in Heaven at the cross and the resurrection of Christ. Paul tells us that Christ disarmed the principalities and made a spectacle of them (see Colossians 2:15). Victory was won in Heaven because of Christ's finished work on the cross. This interpretation fits in with verse 10: *"Then I heard a loud voice in heaven say: 'Now have come the salvation and the power and the kingdom of our God, and the authority of his Christ. For the accuser of our brothers, who accuses them before our God day and night, has been hurled down.' "* The atonement is complete. Forgiveness of sins is now available through the name of Jesus.

Having been hurled down to the earth, Satan is filled with fury (verse 12). What does he do? He turns to attack the woman, who now represents the Church, the new Israel. *"When the dragon saw that he had been hurled to the earth, he pursued the woman who had given birth to the male child"* (verse 13). The woman, the Church, is now under attack from Satan. She flees to the desert for protection.

Christians and the Beasts

Perhaps the two most meaningful verses in chapter 12 are verses 6 and 11. *"The woman fled into the desert to a place prepared for her by God, where she might be taken care of for 1,260 days"* (verse 6). When periods of darkness reigned throughout history, and in the coming final tribulation, the people of God are kept "safe" in the desert. Where is this desert where the Church is protected? What is this desert? We can be reasonably sure that the desert referred to here is not a physical place. We know that the Church does not live in the physical desert. In Revelation 13 to 18, the people of God are being persecuted in the great city where the beast rules. Therefore, we know the desert is not a literal place. It is figurative.

The desert is figurative of the place of rest and nourishment. It is a figurative "place" where God takes care of His own. The term *"desert"* is appropriate because it accurately describes the world in which Christians live. It is called a *"great city"* in Revelation 18, but its true state is that of the wilderness. The *"desert"* therefore is symbolic of a spiritual perspective that sees the world for what it is, the place of wilderness where nothing grows. The physical desert is a place of dryness and where the heat scorches. That is the true state of the world, regardless of appearances. For the woman, the Church, the Christian, there is protection while she maintains this posture of faith and spiritual perspective. Christians will also be nourished spiritually as they seek and commune with God in this environment.

The protection mentioned in verse 6 is not necessarily physical but spiritual, as verse 11 makes clear. *"They overcame him by the blood of the Lamb and by the word of their testimony; they did not love their lives so much as to shrink from death."* The final tribulation is referred to in the 1,260 days. Martyrdom will be the experience of many in those days. They finally overcome by not fearing even death itself. This has been true in the past, and it will apply equally in the future.

In history, there have been shadows of the Great Tribulation. Many tribulation periods have come and gone. The desert principle applies across all ages. We live in the world, but we must understand that at best the world is a spiritual desert where true life is not found. Yet when we see the world in its true form, we shall seek God and find Him. We will worship and commune with Him. We will be nourished spiritually, in the desert. This is never more applicable than when the final Great Tribulation occurs.

The Beasts

Revelation 13:

And the dragon stood on the shore of the sea.

And I saw a beast coming out of the sea. He had ten horns and seven heads, with ten crowns on his horns, and on each head a blasphemous name. {2} The beast I saw resembled a leopard, but had feet like those of a bear and a mouth like that of a lion. The dragon gave the beast his power and his throne and great authority. {3} One of the heads of the beast seemed to have had a fatal wound, but the fatal wound had been healed. The whole world was astonished and followed the beast. {4} Men worshiped the dragon because he had given authority to the beast, and they also worshiped the beast and asked, "Who is like the beast? Who can make war against him?"

{5} The beast was given a mouth to utter proud words and blasphemies and to exercise his authority for forty-two months. {6} He opened his mouth to blaspheme God, and to slander his name and his dwelling place and those who live in heaven. {7} He was given power to make war against the saints and to conquer them. And he was given authority over every tribe, people, language and nation. {8} All inhabitants of the earth will worship the beast — all whose names have not been written in the book of life belonging to the Lamb that was slain from the creation of the world.

{9} He who has an ear, let him hear. {10} If anyone is to go into captivity, into captivity he will go. If anyone is to be killed with the sword, with the sword he will be killed.

This calls for patient endurance and faithfulness on the part of the saints.

{11} Then I saw another beast, coming out of the earth. He had two horns like a lamb, but he spoke like a dragon. {12} He exercised all the authority of the first beast on his behalf, and made the earth and its inhabitants worship the first beast, whose fatal wound had been healed. {13} And he performed

great and miraculous signs, even causing fire to come down from heaven to earth in full view of men. {14} Because of the signs he was given power to do on behalf of the first beast, he deceived the inhabitants of the earth. He ordered them to set up an image in honor of the beast who was wounded by the sword and yet lived. {15} He was given power to give breath to the image of the first beast, so that it could speak and cause all who refused to worship the image to be killed. {16} He also forced everyone, small and great, rich and poor, free and slave, to receive a mark on his right hand or on his forehead, {17} so that no one could buy or sell unless he had the mark, which is the name of the beast or the number of his name.

{18} This calls for wisdom. If anyone has insight, let him calculate the number of the beast, for it is man's number. His number is 666.

We come now to what some consider to be the most interesting, controversial and speculative part of Revelation — chapter 13. The chapter highlights the method or instrument through which Satan now pursues the offspring of the woman, the rest of the Church with her numerous new believers. Two beasts emerged for this purpose. What is the first beast? Some assert it is the future European Union. Others contend it will be a revived Roman Empire. Who is the Antichrist? When Ronald Reagan was president of the United States, some said he was the Antichrist because his middle name also had six letters. Who or what is 666? In the past, some suggested the computer. And what about the Internet? It will greatly assist putting questions such as these in perspective when we ask the broader question: What is the point of chapter 13?

The First Beast:

Let us begin by noting some of the characteristics of the first beast. First, it has ten horns and seven heads. The seven heads represent seven kings, and so do the horns (see Revelation 17:9-12). The numbers ten and seven may not be literal, as they symbolize complete earthly authority. Therefore, the beast is not just one person or one nation.

Second, each head had a blasphemous name. The beast is unashamedly anti-Christian. In John's day, this represented the Roman emperors' claim to deity. For instance, Nero claimed to be "the savior of the world." Third, the beast derived power and authority from Satan (verse 2). It is directly demonic, anti-God and anti-Jesus. Fourth, it has a global following (verses 3-4). It astonished the world because one of its heads (i.e., kings) resembled closely a king of the past. The *"whole world"* followed the beast. Fifth, the beast is worshiped by the world (verses 4 and 8). People also worship the dragon as they worship the beast. The beast is feared by the world because of its military power. The inhabitants of the earth ask: " *'Who is like the beast? Who can make war against him?'* " (verse 4). Sixth, it persecuted Christians (verse 7).

Having looked at the above six characteristics, what might be the identity of the first beast? Daniel 7:17 gives us an important clue, as the four beasts in his vision were four earthly kingdoms. The interpretation was given to him in his vision. Daniel's interpretation is consistent with our six characteristics. The first beast of Revelation is likely to be a political global confederacy of nations which exercises dominion over the whole earth. It has power over all the inhabitants of the earth. Therefore, it is larger than just the European Union. It is not the papacy, as some have claimed, because the beast is political and military in nature. It may not necessarily be a one-world government, as it is more likely to be a confederacy (cf. ten plus seven kings, at least). It is not the United Nations as we presently have it, but the United Nations may be a platform for the beast in the future. This new political confederacy of the future has military power over all, and it is feared by all because of its power of enforcement.

Just as Satan used the beast of the Roman Empire to persecute Christians in the first century, he will use a worldwide political instrument to persecute believers in the final hour. Fifty years ago, it might have seemed unimaginable to have a one-world confederacy. In the early years of the twenty-first century, it is not so difficult to imagine. When the concept of a European community was first suggested twenty years ago, it seemed an impossibility. Now we have the European Union with a common currency. Quite recently, a military force of 60,000 was formed for the European Union. As trading blocks emerge across the globe, it is not hard to imagine some eventual political confederacy consisting of these trading blocks. Even now, Satan is laying the groundwork for the emergence of his first beast — a global instrument for the worldwide persecution of Christians. This hidden motive of the dragon will not be evident until the final hour, when it will be too late to stop him. For the moment, as with the European Union, the reasons for global cooperation will seem legitimate, as they are business related. The issues are initially economic. World trade and a global free market are the present motives for cooperation. But a more sinister mind is behind the present global political and economic forces. It is not a human mind, but a spiritual being called the dragon, Satan himself, preparing the way for the unveiling of his final beast. The human leader of this beast will be the final Antichrist.

The Second Beast:

Now we come to the second beast, which is a derivative of the first. *"Then I saw another beast, coming out of the earth. He had two horns like a lamb, but he spoke like a dragon"* (verse 11). In contrast to the first beast, this one has a gentle, harmless appearance. But we are not to be deceived, as he spoke like a dragon.

Let us consider eight functions of this second beast. First, he exercises full authority on behalf of the first beast. Second, he enforces worship of the first beast. Third, he performs great and miraculous signs publicly. Fourth, he deceives the world through signs. His prime weapon is lies and deception, not brute force. Fifth, he created an image of the first beast for worship. Sixth, he gave life to the image. Seventh, he gave power to the image to kill those who will not worship it. Eighth, he enforces the mark of the first beast upon all who live on the earth.

Who or what is this second beast? He is identified with the false prophet in Revelation 16:13 and 19:20. This second beast is most likely the religious or spiritual arm of the first beast. He has a spiritual and religious role. He deceives through his speech and through false miracles. He is the official representative of the global confederacy. Propaganda is his tool. Public relations is his function. Religion and spirituality is his disguise.

Together with the first beast, what we see here is Satan using the most potent mix of force on the earth to destroy Christians and deceive the world. It is the deadly mixture of politics and religion. We see the power of this combination throughout history. In ancient Egypt, the Pharaohs were supposedly gods. Nebuchadnezzar created a statue of himself and enforced the worship of his image. In John's day, it was the Roman Empire and emperor worship. In Iraq, Saddam Hussein has often called for holy wars. Communism in the past has been enforced as the state religion.

The Mark of the Beast:

What is the mark of the beast which the false prophet enforced? *"He also forced everyone, small and great, rich and poor, free and slave, to receive a mark on his right hand or on his forehead, so that no one could buy or sell unless he had the mark, which is the name of the beast or the number of his name"* (verses 16-17). What is 666?

Three factual points are worth noting at the outset. First, it is the number of the name of the beast. In John's day, Greek alphabets were also used as numbers. Therefore, the Greek version of any name will have a number. This number is given to us: it is 666. Second, no scholar in two thousand years has ever worked out who the number identified in John's day. Some said it was referring to Nero, but this was not even suggested by ancient commentators. Even the famous theologian Irenaeus, a disciple of Polycarp, the bishop of Smyrna, who lived only one hundred years after John, could not work it out. Do we think we can do better, living two thousand years later? Third, John tells us clearly that *it is man's number*. It is the number of "man."

So many through the ages have tried to work out who the number referred to in their day. Even the names of Ronald Reagan and Bill Gates have been suggested in our times. Some claim it is the number representing the computer or the Internet. Others have said it is a computer chip that will be implanted underneath our skin, carrying a computer generated code that will allow us to trade, much like a credit card.

I believe John gave us a very important clue in verse 18: *"This calls for wisdom. If anyone has insight, let him calculate the number of the beast, for it is man's number. His number is 666."* This means the number represents man, or human beings. The thrust is that it does not represent God, who is characterized by the perfect number 7. The number 6 falls short of perfection. The number 666 is the trinity of imperfection. It is the number representing the unholy trinity of the dragon and his two beasts. The number 777 represents God — the Father, the Son, and the Holy Spirit. The number 666 represents Satan, the source of power for the beast and the Antichrist.

John says, *"This calls for wisdom."* Insight is needed not so much to figure out the identity of the beast, but to perceive what the beast represents. Wisdom is needed to know that the leader of this political conglomerate is the Antichrist. He is not a god and does not represent the true God. He is not the Messiah, the Savior. He represents a political force that is the beast of Revelation, whose source is Satan.

Consider it this way: it does not require insight to work out the number of the beast. We are plainly told it is 666. It may not require much wisdom either to identify the mark of the beast. People will not be able to trade without the mark. It is unlikely to be a secret. The identity of the beast is also unlikely to be hidden, given that people will be required to worship its image or be punished. For example, if your government was to enforce putting a mark on your hand without which you cannot buy or sell, and throw you in jail if you confessed to being a Christian, you would not require much insight to know who the beast is. Therefore, insight is necessary not for speculating about what the mark is, but to know what it means and how to respond as Christians when it happens. Wisdom is needed to know that this is what has been prophesied in Revelation, that Christians cannot worship the beast and receive its image, regardless of the cost. It is this that calls for wisdom.

Whether the mark will eventually be represented by a chip implant is anybody's guess. We should not be surprised either way. We need to be mindful that technology is not the problem, but rather who uses it and what it represents. When the beast finally emerges, we will know. His subtlety will be limited. It will also likely be obvious as to what it means to be part of his system. Global persecution of Christians will be occurring. The 'two witnesses' of Revelation 10 would be performing their ministry against the backdrop of deception coming from the second beast. In those days, we need wisdom to know Satan is behind the political conglomerate. *"This calls for patient endurance and faithfulness on the part of the saints"* (verse 10).

Victory and Vindication Assured

Revelation 14:

Then I looked, and there before me was the Lamb, standing on Mount Zion, and with him 144,000 who had his name and his Father's name written on their foreheads. {2} And I heard a sound from heaven like the roar of rushing waters and like a loud peal of thunder. The sound I heard was like that of harpists playing their harps. {3} And they sang a new song before the throne and before the four living creatures and the elders. No one could learn the song except the 144,000 who had been redeemed from the earth. {4} These are those who did not defile themselves with women, for they kept themselves pure. They follow the Lamb wherever he goes. They were purchased from among men and offered as firstfruits to God and the Lamb. {5} No lie was found in their mouths; they are blameless.

{6} Then I saw another angel flying in midair, and he had the eternal gospel to proclaim to those who live on the earth — to every nation, tribe, language and people. {7} He said in a loud voice, "Fear God and give him glory, because the hour of his judgment has come. Worship him who made the heavens, the earth, the sea and the springs of water."

{8} A second angel followed and said, "Fallen! Fallen is Babylon the Great, which made all the nations drink the maddening wine of her adulteries."

{9} A third angel followed them and said in a loud voice: "If anyone worships the beast and his image and receives his mark on the forehead or on the hand, {10} he, too, will drink of the wine of God's fury, which has been poured full strength into the cup of his wrath. He will be tormented with burning sulfur in the presence of the holy angels and of the Lamb. {11} And the smoke of their torment rises for ever and ever. There is no rest day or night for those who worship the beast and his image, or

for anyone who receives the mark of his name." {12} This calls for patient endurance on the part of the saints who obey God's commandments and remain faithful to Jesus.

{13} Then I heard a voice from heaven say, "Write: Blessed are the dead who die in the Lord from now on."

"Yes," says the Spirit, "they will rest from their labor, for their deeds will follow them."

{14} I looked, and there before me was a white cloud, and seated on the cloud was one "like a son of man" with a crown of gold on his head and a sharp sickle in his hand. {15} Then another angel came out of the temple and called in a loud voice to him who was sitting on the cloud, "Take your sickle and reap, because the time to reap has come, for the harvest of the earth is ripe." {16} So he who was seated on the cloud swung his sickle over the earth, and the earth was harvested.

{17} Another angel came out of the temple in heaven, and he too had a sharp sickle. {18} Still another angel, who had charge of the fire, came from the altar and called in a loud voice to him who had the sharp sickle, "Take your sharp sickle and gather the clusters of grapes from the earth's vine, because its grapes are ripe." {19} The angel swung his sickle on the earth, gathered its grapes and threw them into the great winepress of God's wrath. {20} They were trampled in the winepress outside the city, and blood flowed out of the press, rising as high as the horses' bridles for a distance of 1,600 stadia.

The call for endurance is repeated in verse 12 of chapter 14 amid the assurance of victory. The saints are given assurance that the eternal Kingdom will be theirs: *"Then I heard a voice from heaven say, 'Write: Blessed are the dead who die in the Lord from now on.' 'Yes,' says the Spirit, 'they will rest from their labor, for their deeds will follow them' "* (verse 13). Those who have the mark of the beast will be punished by the wrath of God: *" 'If anyone worships the beast and his image and receives his mark on the forehead or on the hand, he, too, will drink of the wine of God's fury, which has been poured full strength into the cup of his wrath. He will be tormented with burning sulfur in the presence of the holy angels and of the*

Lamb. And the smoke of their torment rises for ever and ever. There is no rest day or night for those who worship the beast and his image, or for anyone who receives the mark of his name' " (verses 9-11).

In those days, the ones who overcome will do so *"by the blood of the Lamb and by the word of their testimony; they did not love their lives so much as to shrink from death"* (12:11). This corresponds to the seven short messages to the seven churches, confirming that Revelation is one letter written to all churches — applicable to all Christians throughout history, right to the end of the age. We need to be sure we are growing in those seven vital qualities of an overcomer. The devil is furious because he knows his time is short. But his fury is nothing compared with the wrath of God to come.

Questions for Private Study and Discussion

1. In what way is the woman of Chapter 12 both "old" Israel and "new" Israel (i.e., the Church)?

2. How does the desert perspective provide spiritual nourishment?

3. In what ways is the first beast likely to be a global confederacy of nations?

4. How do wisdom and insight relate to 666?

5. Why would it be obvious *to the Christian* as to what the final beast is when it is revealed?

6. Describe a possible scenario under which the two beasts might emerge. How should Christians behave in such times?

7. How can you apply the overcoming strategy of Revelation 12:11 in your Christian life now?

Chapter 17

FINAL HOUR: THE WRATH OF GOD

Revelation 15:

I saw in heaven another great and marvelous sign: seven angels with the seven last plagues — last, because with them God's wrath is completed. {2} And I saw what looked like a sea of glass mixed with fire and, standing beside the sea, those who had been victorious over the beast and his image and over the number of his name. They held harps given them by God {3} and sang the song of Moses the servant of God and the song of the Lamb: "Great and marvelous are your deeds, Lord God Almighty. Just and true are your ways, King of the ages. {4} Who will not fear you, O Lord, and bring glory to your name? For you alone are holy. All nations will come and worship before you, for your righteous acts have been revealed."

{5} After this I looked and in heaven the temple, that is, the tabernacle of the Testimony, was opened. {6} Out of the temple came the seven angels with the seven plagues. They were dressed in clean, shining linen and wore golden sashes around their chests. {7} Then one of the four living creatures gave to the seven angels seven golden bowls filled with the wrath of God, who lives for ever and ever. {8} And the temple was filled with smoke from the glory of God and from his power, and no one could enter the temple until the seven plagues of the seven angels were completed.

Revelation 16:

Then I heard a loud voice from the temple saying to the seven angels, "Go, pour out the seven bowls of God's wrath on the earth."
{2} The first angel went and poured out his bowl on the land, and ugly and painful sores broke out on the people who had the mark of the beast and worshiped his image.

{3} *The second angel poured out his bowl on the sea, and it turned into blood like that of a dead man, and every living thing in the sea died.*
{4} *The third angel poured out his bowl on the rivers and springs of water, and they became blood. {5} Then I heard the angel in charge of the waters say:*

"You are just in these judgments, you who are and who were, the Holy One, because you have so judged; {6} for they have shed the blood of your saints and prophets, and you have given them blood to drink as they deserve."
{7} *And I heard the altar respond:*

"Yes, Lord God Almighty, true and just are your judgments."
{8} *The fourth angel poured out his bowl on the sun, and the sun was given power to scorch people with fire. {9} They were seared by the intense heat and they cursed the name of God, who had control over these plagues, but they refused to repent and glorify him.*
{10} *The fifth angel poured out his bowl on the throne of the beast, and his kingdom was plunged into darkness. Men gnawed their tongues in agony {11} and cursed the God of heaven because of their pains and their sores, but they refused to repent of what they had done.*
{12} *The sixth angel poured out his bowl on the great river Euphrates, and its water was dried up to prepare the way for the kings from the East. {13} Then I saw three evil spirits that looked like frogs; they came out of the mouth of the dragon, out of the mouth of the beast and out of the mouth of the false prophet. {14} They are spirits of demons performing miraculous signs, and they go out to the kings of the whole world, to gather them for the battle on the great day of God Almighty.*
{15} *"Behold, I come like a thief! Blessed is he who stays awake and keeps his clothes with him, so that he may not go naked and be shamefully exposed."*
{16} *Then they gathered the kings together to the place that in Hebrew is called Armageddon.*
{17} *The seventh angel poured out his bowl into the air, and out of the temple came a loud voice from the throne, saying, "It is done!"*
{18} *Then there came flashes of lightning, rumblings, peals of thun-*

der and a severe earthquake. No earthquake like it has ever occurred since man has been on earth, so tremendous was the quake. {19} The great city split into three parts, and the cities of the nations collapsed. God remembered Babylon the Great and gave her the cup filled with the wine of the fury of his wrath. {20} Every island fled away and the mountains could not be found. {21} From the sky huge hailstones of about a hundred pounds each fell upon men. And they cursed God on account of the plague of hail, because the plague was so terrible.

We are almost approaching the end, although the climax relating to the world financial system is still two chapters away in Revelation 17 and 18. For the purposes of this book, there are only four chapters left. They will cover the eight remaining chapters of Revelation. In the two chapters we will consider here, the wrath of God is in focus. The seven bowls represent nothing less than God's wrath, poured out in righteous anger against extreme evil. They are fundamentally different from the seven seals and trumpets considered earlier in that they issue from God's very presence. The Battle of Armageddon is also mentioned here, and it will be interpreted simply and meaningfully.

Introduction to the Bowls

Chapter 15 is the shortest chapter in the book of Revelation. Although it serves as an introduction to chapter 16, it is an important prelude. It communicates a very important point: that the bowls represent God's direct judgment of and intervention in the affairs of man and earth.

The seven bowls of wrath issue from the very presence of the Almighty One. *"And the temple was filled with smoke from the glory of God and from his power, and no one could enter the temple until the seven plagues of the seven angels were completed"* (verse 8). The glory of God filling the heavenly Temple reminds us of Moses' encounters with God in the Old Testament. The glory and smoke filling the Temple communicates the manifestation of the awesome presence of God. The seven angels emerged from the Temple (verse 6) and were handed seven bowls (verse 7). The wrath of God had to be completed before anyone could reenter the Temple. The original concept of completion in verses 1 and 8 means "to conclude or to fulfill." Thus, no one is allowed to even intercede before God until the seven plagues are concluded. We should remind ourselves that the judgment of God is partly in response to the prayers of the martyrs for justice.

The world as it is will end. There will be a conclusion to all of the confusion and madness we see in the world today. Are you glad that there is a conclusion to the insanity we see in the world? It is a world where genocide occurs and where there is great economic divide between the rich and the poor. It is a world where child labor abounds and where girls are forced into prostitution just to stay alive. The list could go on, but by the twenty-first century many are already familiar with the atrocities of humanity.

It is worth noting that not only will there be an end, but there will be a new beginning. It is not the end of the world with no new beginnings. That would be most tragic indeed. The new beginning, however, will be predicated upon the end. This present world needs to end, so that the new can commence. Further, not only will there be an end but there would be justice. Yes, mercy goes before and is available through Christ, but justice will be meted out. Evil will be punished. We should expect nothing less from a just God.

The Seven Bowls

We turn now to the seven bowls described in chapter 16. *"Then I heard a loud voice from the temple saying to the seven angels, 'Go, pour out the seven bowls of God's wrath on the earth' "* (verse 1). What are these bowls? What do they represent? Are Christians immune from their effects?

"The first angel went and poured out his bowl on the land, and ugly and painful sores broke out on the people who had the mark of the beast and worshiped his image" (verse 2). This verse tells us two important things. First, the painful sores only affect those who have the mark of the beast. In other words, believers are immune from these plagues. The entire experience will be nothing less than miraculous, just as at the time of Moses in Egypt when only the firstborn of all Egyptians were slain but the Israelites were spared. Second, verse 2 indicates that Christians are

still around throughout the world. They have not been raptured. Neither is there any evidence to suggest that these are only new believers or Jewish believers. Christians of all nationalities escape the wrath of God miraculously even as they are being martyred by man.

The first four bowls are poured on the earth, sea, rivers and sun respectively. A few points are worth noting in comparison to the first four trumpets of chapters 8 and 9. Both trumpets and bowls represent the destruction of nature, with serious consequences for mankind. For instance, the waters are poisoned and marine life is damaged. There are two major differences, however. First, with the trumpets only a third of creation is destroyed, whereas with the bowls, the destruction is total. Second, the bowls represent the direct judgment of God. This point is repeated throughout the chapter, for instance in verse 7: *"And I heard the altar respond: 'Yes, Lord God Almighty, true and just are your judgments.'"* It seems as though nature is being employed to yield maximum damage to mankind. In the fourth bowl, the heat of the sun is turned up, so to speak: *"The fourth angel poured out his bowl on the sun, and the sun was given power to scorch people with fire. They were seared by the intense heat and they cursed the name of God, who had control over these plagues, but they refused to repent and glorify him"* (verses 8-9).

How do the seals of chapters 6, the trumpets of chapters 8 and 9, and these bowls of chapter 16 relate to each other? As the following diagram illustrates, they expand with greater detail as we approach the second coming of Christ. The trumpets (which the seventh seal unfolds) offer greater detail of the sixth seal, and the bowls give more information concerning the very end.

The fifth bowl is poured onto the throne of the beast: *"The fifth angel poured out his bowl on the throne of the beast, and his kingdom was plunged into darkness"* (verse 10). The results are chaos and disorder in the empire. The curse of God will continue, as there will be little repentance. In hatred and revenge, the inhabitants of the earth will keep martyring Christians as they are inspired by the dragon to do.

The sixth bowl concerns Armageddon. In this bowl, frogs, demons, the dragon, the beast, the false prophet and kings are all involved. *"The sixth angel poured out his bowl on the great river Euphrates, and its water was dried up to prepare the way for the kings from the East. Then I saw three evil spirits that looked like frogs; they came out of the mouth of the dragon, out of the mouth of the beast and out of the mouth of the false prophet"* (verses 12-13). What do these evil spirits do? What is their primary function at this juncture of time? They continue the work of deception and now gather the leaders of the world for the battle of Armageddon: *"They are spirits of demons performing miraculous signs, and they go out to the*

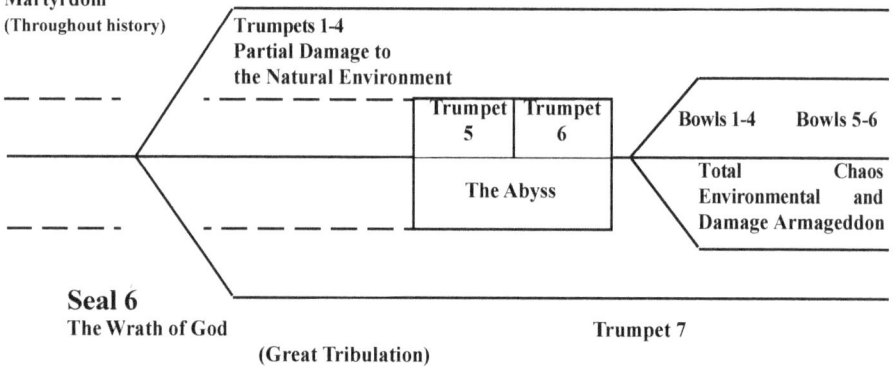

kings of the whole world, to gather them for the battle on the great day of God Almighty" (verse 14).

What is the Battle of Armageddon? As some of us are aware, there has been no shortage of speculation involved in this matter. Will Russia invade Israel, as some have suggested from their interpretation of Gog and Magog (Revelation 20)? Will there be World War III in Palestine? I think a few clues will help us understand Armageddon better. First, *"Armageddon"* in the Hebrew language means "mount of Megiddo." However, there is no actual Mount Megiddo to be found anywhere on earth. Many interpretations have been given concerning where and what Mount Megiddo is. Some say it refers to the hill country near Megiddo. Others contend that it is Megiddo itself. Some interpret it as the mount of assembly, while others argue it is symbolic of a destroying mountain. Therefore, as a physical location, there is no mount of Megiddo.

The second clue is to be found in Megiddo itself. The foot of Megiddo is a place where many decisive battles in the Old Testament were fought and kings were killed. For example, the kings Saul, Josiah and Ahaziah were killed there. Deborah fought a decisive battle there. It is symbolic of the final and greatest of all battles.

The third clue is in verse 16: *"Then they gathered the kings together to the place that in Hebrew is called Armageddon."* The same is said in verse 14, where the evil spirits gather the leaders of the world for the final battle against God: *"and they go out to the kings of the whole world, to gather them for the battle on the great day of God Almighty."* This third clue is in fact decisive and offers us a clear indication of what Armageddon is. It is *"the battle on the great day of God Almighty."* Putting all these clues together tells us that geography is not the issue here. The issue is what Armageddon has come to symbolize: great decisive battles. It is a most appropriate symbol for the great and final battle between good and evil, between God and Satan. It will happen on the Day of the Lord. It will be the final hour, and it will occur at the final minute to mark the end of time itself.

The seventh bowl confirms the interpretation above. What is the last and final bowl? It is the Second Coming, the appearing of Jesus Christ in the clouds: *"The seventh angel poured out his bowl into the air, and out of the temple came a loud voice from the throne, saying, 'It is done!' "* (verse 17). With the coming of Christ are *"flashes of lightning, rumblings, peals of thunder and a severe earthquake. No earthquake like it has ever occurred since man has been on earth, so tremendous was the quake"* (verse 18). But more needs to be said in the next two chapters concerning Babylon before this battle is eventually described to us.

Conclusion

To conclude, we must pick up verse 15. There Jesus says, *"Behold, I come like a thief! Blessed is he who stays awake and keeps his clothes with him, so that he may not go naked and be shamefully exposed."* This is the most important verse in the chapter. It is the practical application and the personal exhortation of Christ for us. He exhorted the disciples in such a way while He was on earth. Now He repeats it here, in the context of the very end before He comes again. We need to stay awake and be watchful, or risk being indecently exposed. When the world is collapsing around us, we need to stand firm and lift up our heads, for our redemption is drawing near.

Questions for Private Study and Discussion

1. How does chapter 15 communicate to us that the bowls are the wrath of God?

2. How should we respond to the fact that there is a conclusion to all the "insanity" we see in our world?

3. How do the series of seals, trumpets and bowls relate to each other?

4. What do you think of the author's interpretation of Armageddon? What are the advantages of this interpretation?

5. In what ways can we "stay awake" as Christians?

Chapter 18

ECONOMIC ZONE: THE LAST BABYLON

Revelation 17:

> One of the seven angels who had the seven bowls came and said to me, "Come, I will show you the punishment of the great prostitute, who sits on many waters. {2} With her the kings of the earth committed adultery and the inhabitants of the earth were intoxicated with the wine of her adulteries."
>
> {3} Then the angel carried me away in the Spirit into a desert. There I saw a woman sitting on a scarlet beast that was covered with blasphemous names and had seven heads and ten horns. {4} The woman was dressed in purple and scarlet, and was glittering with gold, precious stones and pearls. She held a golden cup in her hand, filled with abominable things and the filth of her adulteries. {5} This title was written on her forehead:
>
> MYSTERY BABYLON THE GREAT THE MOTHER OF PROSTITUTES AND OF THE ABOMINATIONS OF THE EARTH.
>
> {6} I saw that the woman was drunk with the blood of the saints, the blood of those who bore testimony to Jesus.
>
> When I saw her, I was greatly astonished. {7} Then the angel said to me: "Why are you astonished? I will explain to you the mystery of the woman and of the beast she rides, which has the seven heads and ten horns. {8} The beast, which you saw, once was, now is not, and will come up out of the Abyss and go to his destruction. The inhabitants of the earth whose names have not been written in the book of life from the creation of the world will be astonished when they see the beast, because he once was, now is not, and yet will come.

{9} *"This calls for a mind with wisdom. The seven heads are seven hills on which the woman sits. {10} They are also seven kings. Five have fallen, one is, the other has not yet come; but when he does come, he must remain for a little while. {11} The beast who once was, and now is not, is an eighth king. He belongs to the seven and is going to his destruction.*

{12} *"The ten horns you saw are ten kings who have not yet received a kingdom, but who for one hour will receive authority as kings along with the beast. {13} They have one purpose and will give their power and authority to the beast. {14} They will make war against the Lamb, but the Lamb will overcome them because he is Lord of lords and King of kings — and with him will be his called, chosen and faithful followers."*

{15} *Then the angel said to me, "The waters you saw, where the prostitute sits, are peoples, multitudes, nations and languages. {16} The beast and the ten horns you saw will hate the prostitute. They will bring her to ruin and leave her naked; they will eat her flesh and burn her with fire. {17} For God has put it into their hearts to accomplish his purpose by agreeing to give the beast their power to rule, until God's words are fulfilled. {18} The woman you saw is the great city that rules over the kings of the earth."*

Revelation 18:

After this I saw another angel coming down from heaven. He had great authority, and the earth was illuminated by his splendor. {2} With a mighty voice he shouted:

"Fallen! Fallen is Babylon the Great! She has become a home for demons and a haunt for every evil spirit, a haunt for every unclean and detestable bird. {3} For all the nations have drunk the maddening wine of her adulteries. The kings of the earth committed adultery with her, and the merchants of the earth grew rich from her excessive luxuries."

{4} *Then I heard another voice from heaven say:*

"Come out of her, my people, so that you will not share in her sins, so that you will not receive any of her plagues; {5} for her sins are piled up to heaven, and God has remembered her crimes. {6} Give

back to her as she has given; pay her back double for what she has done. Mix her a double portion from her own cup. {7} Give her as much torture and grief as the glory and luxury she gave herself. In her heart she boasts, 'I sit as queen; I am not a widow, and I will never mourn.' {8} Therefore in one day her plagues will overtake her: death, mourning and famine. She will be consumed by fire, for mighty is the Lord God who judges her.

{9} "When the kings of the earth who committed adultery with her and shared her luxury see the smoke of her burning, they will weep and mourn over her. {10} Terrified at her torment, they will stand far off and cry:

" 'Woe! Woe, O great city, O Babylon, city of power! In one hour your doom has come!' {11} "The merchants of the earth will weep and mourn over her because no one buys their cargoes any more — {12} cargoes of gold, silver, precious stones and pearls; fine linen, purple, silk and scarlet cloth; every sort of citron wood, and articles of every kind made of ivory, costly wood, bronze, iron and marble; {13} cargoes of cinnamon and spice, of incense, myrrh and frankincense, of wine and olive oil, of fine flour and wheat; cattle and sheep; horses and carriages; and bodies and souls of men. {14} "They will say, 'The fruit you longed for is gone from you. All your riches and splendor have vanished, never to be recovered.' {15} The merchants who sold these things and gained their wealth from her will stand far off, terrified at her torment. They will weep and mourn {16} and cry out:

" 'Woe! Woe, O great city, dressed in fine linen, purple and scarlet, and glittering with gold, precious stones and pearls! {17} In one hour such great wealth has been brought to ruin!'

"Every sea captain, and all who travel by ship, the sailors, and all who earn their living from the sea, will stand far off. {18} When they see the smoke of her burning, they will exclaim, 'Was there ever a city like this great city?' {19} They will throw dust on their heads, and with weeping and mourning cry out: "'Woe! Woe, O great city, where all who had ships on the sea became rich through her wealth! In one hour she has been brought to ruin! {20} Rejoice over her, O heaven! Rejoice,

saints and apostles and prophets! God has judged her for the way she treated you.' "
{21} Then a mighty angel picked up a boulder the size of a large millstone and threw it into the sea, and said:
"With such violence the great city of Babylon will be thrown down, never to be found again. {22} The music of harpists and musicians, flute players and trumpeters, will never be heard in you again. No workman of any trade will ever be found in you again. The sound of a millstone will never be heard in you again. {23} The light of a lamp will never shine in you again. The voice of bridegroom and bride will never be heard in you again. Your merchants were the world's great men. By your magic spell all the nations were led astray. {24} In her was found the blood of prophets and of the saints, and of all who have been killed on the earth."

I hope we can see by now that it is not too difficult to grasp the main messages of Revelation. It is basically a pastoral letter to encourage and exhort Christians. It highlights both the vital role of the Church in her persevering witness for Christ until the very end, and the sovereignty of God in spite of the chaos of evil. It provides hope for the darkest period of human history.

The Apocalypse is increasingly relevant as we enter further into a new century. The volatility of our world makes the fulfillment of all these prophecies possible within thirty years. Consider the following: Hitler became a power to be reckoned with within just a few short years in the 1930s. Hitler can be considered a shadow of the final Antichrist, even as many Antichrists have come and gone. The strange thing was that he was almost an unknown before 1930. But in a very short time he rose to prominence and power. The point is that things can happen quickly. Two world wars were fought within a span of thirty years in the last century.

No one knows for sure what will happen in the future. What we do know is that the world is changing faster than we can comprehend. As we all know, technological changes have shrunk the globe through improved aviation and better communication. The fact that this book is available over the Internet is a case in point. Even the global environment is changing. There is now scientific evidence that world climate has changed more in the twentieth century than the past nineteen hundred years combined. The drive for world trade is fueling global cooperation like never before. Who would have thought that the European Union could come together so quickly and with a common currency?

None of what I have written above is exaggerated in any way. The plain statement of facts together with a simple but meaningful interpretation of Revelation is like putting a match to gasoline. Without being dogmatic or overly simplistic, it is well possible that these prophecies can be fulfilled in our lifetime. The chapters we are about to consider should no less heighten that sense of urgency.

Desert Insight

Chapters 17 and 18 talk about the last Babylon, the mother of all prostitutes. They tell us of her relationship with the beast and of her eventual destruction. More importantly, Christ gave an exhortation to the Church as to how we should behave when the time comes for the punishment of the great prostitute. Then, it will be a time of physical separation. Now we are to practice a form of spiritual separation. More will be explained later. I am not saying we should all go live in a monastery.

Let us begin with verse 1 and 2 of chapter 17: *"One of the seven angels who had the seven bowls came and said to me, 'Come, I will show you the punishment of the great prostitute, who sits on many waters. With her the kings of the earth committed adultery and the inhabitants of the earth were intoxicated with the wine of her adulteries.'"* This tells us immediately the purpose of this new scene, which is to show us the punishment of the great prostitute.

Verse 3 is important, as it tells us where John was carried by the Spirit in order that he may see the prostitute for who she really is. Where might that place of perspective be? *"Then the angel carried me away in the Spirit into a desert."* Once again, the desert perspective is mentioned. It is in the "wilderness" that we see the truth from God's viewpoint. *"There I saw a woman sitting on a scarlet beast that was covered with blasphemous names and had seven heads and ten horns."* There is an important lesson for us here. If we are not seeing the prostitute for who she really is, we are probably not in the right place spiritually. We need to learn the principle of spiritual separation, that we might cultivate the desert perspective and perceive the truth.

Seven Features of the Prostitute

Who is the prostitute? What are her features? Surely we are to know because we are commanded to *"come out of her."* We are not to be part of her, so that we will not share in her plagues. But that assumes we know who she is!

Let us then consider her features, before we come to her identity:

First, she is extremely wealthy. *"The woman was dressed in purple and scarlet, and was glittering with gold, precious stones and pearls"* (17:4). She is excessively rich. The merchants of the earth grew rich from her *"excessive luxuries"* (18:3 and 12).

Second, she has great influence. This global influence is in two major arenas: economics and culture. In economics, she is a leader in commerce: *"Your merchants were the world's great men"* (18:23). Babylon the prostitute is inhabited by world-renowned businesspeople. She will own the best businesses in the world and possess the best graduate schools of management. In popular culture she leads the world: *"The inhabitants of the earth were intoxicated with the wine of her adulteries"* (17:2). *"By your magic spell all the nations were led astray"* (18:23). She is immoral, degenerate and highly hedonistic. *"She held a golden cup in her hand, filled with abominable things and the filth of her adulteries"* (17:4).

The prostitute has tremendous influence over two groups of people. The first is world leaders: *"The kings of the earth committed adultery with her"* (18:3). Her dominance is through economic might and not through military power. She is a powerful trading partner. The second group is people all over the world: *"The waters you saw, where the prostitute sits, are peoples, multitudes, nations and languages"* (17:15).

Third, the prostitute is an adulteress and extremely sinful (17:2 and 18:3 and 9). Prominent politicians commit adultery with her by trading with her and participating in her sins.

Fourth, she gives birth to other prostitutes. She is *"MYSTERY BABYLON THE GREAT, THE MOTHER OF PROSTITUTES AND OF THE ABOMINATIONS OF THE EARTH"* (17:5). In other words, her "success" is emulated elsewhere in the world. Others want to become like her.

Fifth, she is the city of Babylon. *"This title was written on her forehead: MYSTERY BABYLON THE GREAT THE MOTHER OF PROSTITUTES ..."* (17:5). Therefore, the woman in these two chapters is the great prostitute who is also the great city of Babylon. Babylon in the Old Testament has come to symbolize the enemy of God.

Sixth, and perhaps the most important, Christians die by her hands. *"In her was found the blood of prophets and of the saints, and of all who have been killed on the earth"* (18:24). She is not the beast, but she too persecutes Christians. *"I saw that the woman was drunk with the blood of the saints, the blood of those who bore testimony to Jesus. When I saw her, I was greatly astonished"* (17:6). Perhaps the prostitute has something significant to do with the mark of the beast, without which none can trade. This is also a clear confirmation that Christians are still around all over the world, as they are being martyred. They have not been raptured.

Seventh, the prostitute has an uneasy, love-hate relationship with the beast. *"The beast and the ten horns you saw will hate the prostitute. They will bring her to ruin and leave her naked; they will eat her flesh and burn her with fire"* (17:16). This is an important point to keep in mind. It tells us that the beast is likely to be a loose conglomerate of nations and not so much a one-world government. The beast and the prostitute hate each other, but they will cooperate to torture and kill Christians. They are united against the risen Lamb.

The Identity of Babylon

What is the identity of Babylon? The seven features mentioned above will greatly assist us in identifying the last Babylon when the time comes. Before the final hour, there have been many shadow Babylons that have come and gone, just as many shadow Antichrists have gone into the world. The apostle John would have identified the

Roman Empire to be the Babylon of his day. Rome was very wealthy and had numerous volunteer colonies. She also persecuted Christians. In John's day, the beast and Babylon both happened to be the Roman Empire. This will probably not be the case for the final hour.

What about those of us who are living in the early twenty-first century? Is there a type of Babylon existing in our day, even if she is not the final Babylon? Is there a country that is economically powerful and culturally influential? Is it possible to say that the United States might be a precursor to what is to come? No, I am not at all asserting that the U.S.A. is the final Babylon. America is not involved in the persecution of Christians, which is a vital feature for identifying the final prostitute. However, some other features do have resemblances. The U.S. is the world's economic powerhouse, possessing the best multinational companies. The rest of the world is made wealthy through trading with her and learning from her. She has the most powerful stock market in the world. As the saying goes, "When Wall Street sneezes, the world catches a cold." The United States has great cultural influence in terms of popular culture. Think of the spread of cultural products such as Coke, McDonald's, Hollywood movies, pop music and philosophical values inherent in postmodernism. This is not to deny that there has also been much good arising out of the United States — for example her pursuit of democratic freedom and her technological advances.

The only thing presently preventing the U.S. from being a Babylon is that she is not martyring Christians. She is *not* the enemy of God. But changes could happen quickly. Remember how fast Hitler rose to power in Germany. If America ever begins to persecute Christians, we will know that she has begun evolving into a full-fledged Babylon. Does anyone know for sure what the United States might be like thirty years from now? Will she still have a God-fearing President as she does now? If you are an American reader, please do not take offense, as I am not at all anti-American.

What about other possibilities? Some have said that Babylon is the Roman Catholic Church. I do not find this convincing because the Roman Catholic Church is not an economic superpower. Others have suggested that Babylon is an ideology, such as capitalism. However,

Economic Zone: The Last Babylon

I think the final Babylon will be much less abstract than an ideology. A well-respected commentator interprets Babylon as "civilized man ordering society apart from God," that it is symbolic of the world. While this has some merits, once again I think the last prostitute will be less abstract and more readily identifiable.

The final Babylon will probably be a country or a region that is the dominant economic power of the world exercising great influence over the way business is done. It will be involved in martyring Christians. It is likely to be closely connected with the mark of the beast, whatever that may be. It is worth noting that the primary motivating force behind the European Union, GATT, NAFTA, APEC, and the WTO is commerce. The emergence of a global stock market where people can trade anytime and anywhere is also a relevant phenomenon to be watched, as we shall see in the next section.

The Destruction of Babylon

When the final Babylon raises her head, we are commanded to come out of her. We are not to take part in her adulterous activity. Revelation tells us that Babylon will be destroyed, and chapter 18 shows us how that will happen.

Babylon will be destroyed by the beast: *"The beast and the ten horns you saw will hate the prostitute. They will bring her to ruin and leave her naked; they will eat her flesh and burn her with fire"* (17:16). It will happen suddenly and speedily. It will happen in *"one hour"*: *"They will throw dust on their heads, and with weeping and mourning cry out: 'Woe! Woe, O great city, where all who had ships on the sea became rich through her wealth! In one hour she has been brought to ruin!' "* (18:19). I do not think it is referring to a literal sixty-minute hour, but it will be swift: *"Therefore in one day her plagues will overtake her: death, mourning and famine"* (18:8).

The prostitute's ruin will also be violent: *"Then a mighty angel picked up a boulder the size of a large millstone and threw it into the sea, and said: 'With such violence the great city of Babylon will be thrown down, never to be found again' "* (18:21). She will be burned and destroyed, according to the divine intervention of God through natural means: *"They will bring her to ruin and leave her naked; they will eat her flesh and burn her with fire. For God has put it into their hearts to accomplish his purpose by agreeing to give the beast their power to rule, until God's words are fulfilled"* (17:16-17).

The destruction of Babylon will result in worldwide economic chaos. It will result in the collapse of financial systems around the world. *"The merchants of the earth will weep and mourn over her because no one buys their cargoes any more"* (18:11). Imagine what would happen if the top one hundred companies of the world were to suddenly collapse in our day? What would that do to the equity markets around the world? The Dow Jones Industrial Average might fall by ninety percent, the Nasdaq would plunge, and along with that, Japan's Nikkei, Hong Kong's Hang Seng and Australia's All Ordinary Index. The Asian financial crisis of 1997 and the crash of 1987 will pale into insignificance compared with the collapse of the last Babylon. It will happen suddenly and swiftly.

It is the beast that destroys Babylon. As mentioned previously, they have a love-hate relationship. Even the beast itself is fragmented from within. The leaders of this conglomerate of nations do not really get along (17:10-13). Some will receive power only for a short time. This indicates that the beast is unlikely to be a one-world government, but a loose confederacy of self-interested nations. Nevertheless, the beast detests Babylon, the rich prostitute. It is a little bit like Iraq hating the United States, if that will help us imagine how the future might occur. I like the way Revelation plays out here — it matches the confusing and often opposing forces at work in the real world. These prophecies are realistic and credible. Our interpretations should be no less. Truth and reality are often paradoxical in nature. For example, the beast is a king (a leader) as well as a confederacy: *"The beast who once was, and now is not, is an eighth king. He belongs to the seven and is going to his destruction"* (17:11). The political leader of the beastly alliance will be the Antichrist.

By the way, for those who like complexity, it could be that John took the *"seven hills on which the woman sits"* (17:9) to refer to Rome, for the seven hills of that city are often mentioned in ancient literature. *"They are also seven kings. Five have fallen, one is, the other has not yet come; but when he does come, he must remain for a little while"* (17:10). On this verse I prefer Hendriksen's interpretation of seeing the kings as representative of five empires that have fallen: the Old Babylonian, the Assyrian, the New Babylonian, the Medo-Persian and the Greco-Macedonian. The "one that is" was the Roman Empire of John's day. The seventh is in the future. But regardless of the specifics, the basic point is clear: there have been shadows of the beast throughout history, yet the final one to come is most horrific. We thought that such things would not occur again *("the beast who once was")*, but when they do, we will be astonished *("yet will come")*.

I maintain that by the time these prophecies are fulfilled, it should be obvious to Christians what the beast is. The identity of the final Babylon will also be clear. The beast is not subtle. You will know when you are being persecuted and martyred! Nonbelievers will be deceived as to its true nature, that it is energized by the dragon against God. But Christians are to be wise, as they have been forewarned. The deception of the false prophet (the second beast of chapter 13) works on nonbelievers, but it is not supposed to affect Christians. We are not to be deceived along with the rest of the world. That is why Jesus said, *"Blessed is he who keeps the words of the prophecy in this book"* (22:7).

Conclusion

The exhortation Christ gave to those confronting the last Babylon is in 18:4, *"Come out of her, my people, so that you will not share in her sins, so that you will not receive any of her plagues."* When the time comes, we are not to receive the mark of the beast or participate with Babylon. None can trade or do business without the mark; therefore, the mark must be required for trading with Babylon. Christians are not to engage the prostitute. We are to come out of her. Separation of some sort will be necessary. It means not being part of that system and not receiving the mark.

What about those of us who are not yet living in those times when the beast and Babylon are revealed? We can practice spiritual separation now. No, it does not mean we quit our jobs or sell our house and go live in a monastery. As John's epistle exhorts, we are to be in the world but not of it. It does not mean we shouldn't use our credit cards or that we should dispose of our investments. It means that our treasures are not on earth and that our values are not of this world. It means that our priorities are Kingdom priorities, such as the Great Commission and the first commandment. Augustine put it this way: "We must renounce our rights as citizens of this world, and flee unto God on the wings of faith."

Questions for Private Study and Discussion

1. What are the seven features of the last Babylon?

2. How does the prostitute exercise influence?

3. Why is it that no country on earth fits the description of Babylon totally at this stage of the twenty-first century?

4. What do you think of the author's interpretation concerning the identity of the final Babylon?

5. How will the prostitute be destroyed?

6. What does it mean to "come out of" Babylon? How can the principle of separation be applied now?

Chapter 19

BEYOND 2000:
THE MILLENNIUM INTERPRETED

Revelation 19:

After this I heard what sounded like the roar of a great multitude in heaven shouting:

"Hallelujah! Salvation and glory and power belong to our God, {2} for true and just are his judgments. He has condemned the great prostitute who corrupted the earth by her adulteries. He has avenged on her the blood of his servants."

{3} And again they shouted: "Hallelujah! The smoke from her goes up for ever and ever."

{4} The twenty-four elders and the four living creatures fell down and worshiped God, who was seated on the throne. And they cried: "Amen, Hallelujah!"

{5} Then a voice came from the throne, saying:

"Praise our God, all you his servants, you who fear him, both small and great!"

{6} Then I heard what sounded like a great multitude, like the roar of rushing waters and like loud peals of thunder, shouting:

"Hallelujah! For our Lord God Almighty reigns. {7} Let us rejoice and be glad and give him glory! For the wedding of the Lamb has come, and his bride has made herself ready. {8} Fine linen, bright and clean, was given her to wear."

(Fine linen stands for the righteous acts of the saints.)

{9} Then the angel said to me, "Write: 'Blessed are those who are invited to the wedding supper of the Lamb!'" And he added, "These are the true words of God."

{10} At this I fell at his feet to worship him. But he said to me, "Do not do it! I am a fellow servant with you and with your brothers who hold to the testimony of Jesus. Worship God! For the testimony of Jesus is the spirit of prophecy."

{11} I saw heaven standing open and there before me was a white horse, whose rider is called Faithful and True. With justice he judges and makes war. {12} His eyes are like blazing fire, and on his head are many crowns. He has a name written on him that no one knows but he himself. {13} He is dressed in a robe dipped in blood, and his name is the Word of God. {14} The armies of heaven were following him, riding on white horses and dressed in fine linen, white and clean. {15} Out of his mouth comes a sharp sword with which to strike down the nations. "He will rule them with an iron scepter." He treads the winepress of the fury of the wrath of God Almighty. {16} On his robe and on his thigh he has this name written: KING OF KINGS AND LORD OF LORDS.

{17} And I saw an angel standing in the sun, who cried in a loud voice to all the birds flying in midair, "Come, gather together for the great supper of God, {18} so that you may eat the flesh of kings, generals, and mighty men, of horses and their riders, and the flesh of all people, free and slave, small and great."

{19} Then I saw the beast and the kings of the earth and their armies gathered together to make war against the rider on the horse and his army. {20} But the beast was captured, and with him the false prophet who had performed the miraculous signs on his behalf. With these signs he had deluded those who had received the mark of the beast and worshiped his image. The two of them were thrown alive into the fiery lake of burning sulfur. {21} The rest of them were killed with the sword that came out of the mouth of the rider on the horse, and all the birds gorged themselves on their flesh.

We are approaching the very end. Now the devil himself, that horrendous dragon, will be judged. That is in chapter 20. We will move through chapter 19 quickly, as the message is straightforward even as it deals with the outcome of Armageddon. Chapter 20 will be more complex and controversial, as it deals with the thousand years. Is the millennial reign of Christ literal or symbolic? We shall see.

King of Kings and Lord of Lords

The first ten verses of chapter 19 are the Hallelujah Chorus. Praise is offered to God for four things. First, God is praised for His judgment on the prostitute, Babylon. The blood of the martyrs is avenged. Second, God is praised for His sovereign reign throughout the Great Tribulation. Despite the darkness, God was in control. Third, the wedding supper of the Lamb has finally arrived. Christians through the ages have been waiting for this moment. Fourth, the Bride of Christ, the Church, has made herself ready. This is a pointed reminder for us all that when Christ finally comes again, He will be looking for those who are spiritually prepared.

The Hallelujah Chorus leads us into the next section (verses 11-16) when the heavenly bridegroom arrives with the armies of Heaven. It describes the One who comes on a white horse. He has three names. He is Faithful and True, in contrast to the deceiving dragon. He is the Word of God, as the gospel of John testifies. He is also the King of kings and the Lord of lords. As we can see, He is none other than Jesus Christ, our Savior and Lord.

The remainder of the chapter reveals the outcome of Armageddon, where the Antichrist and his allies are gathered for the battle of the Day of the Lord. *"Then I saw the beast and the kings of the earth and their armies gathered together to make war against the rider on the horse and his army"* (verse 19). Remember what we said about Armageddon. It represents the greatest battle between good and evil, between God and Satan. It is as if the nations of the world have conspired to wipe out Christians from the face of the globe in one final effort. The final battle, however, will be an anti-climax. The beast, that confederacy of nations led by the Antichrist, and the false prophet, were simply captured and *"thrown alive into the fiery lake of burning sulfur"* (verse 20). The final battle will be no battle at all. It will not be a war lasting weeks or months. When Christ appears, the beast will simply melt in the fire of His judgment: *"Out of his mouth comes a sharp sword with which to strike down the nations. 'He will rule them with an iron scepter.' He treads the winepress of the fury of the wrath of God Almighty"* (verse 15).

The Thousand Years

Revelation 20:

And I saw an angel coming down out of heaven, having the key to the Abyss and holding in his hand a great chain. {2} He seized the dragon, that ancient serpent, who is the devil, or Satan, and bound him for a thousand years. {3} He threw him into the Abyss, and locked and sealed it over him, to keep him from deceiving the nations anymore until the thousand years were ended. After that, he must be set free for a short time.

{4} I saw thrones on which were seated those who had been given authority to judge. And I saw the souls of those who had been beheaded because of their testimony for Jesus and because of the word of God. They had not worshiped the beast or his image and had not received his mark on their foreheads or their hands. They came to life and reigned with Christ a thousand years. {5} (The rest of the dead did not come to life until the thousand years were ended.) This is the first resurrection. {6} Blessed and holy are those who have part in the first resurrection. The second death has no power over them, but they will be priests of God and of Christ and will reign with him for a thousand years.

{7} When the thousand years are over, Satan will be released from his prison {8} and will go out to deceive the nations in the four corners of the earth — Gog and Magog — to gather them for battle. In number they are like the sand on the seashore. {9} They marched across the breadth of the earth and surrounded the camp of God's people, the city he loves. But fire came down from heaven and devoured them. {10} And the devil, who deceived them, was thrown into the lake of burning sulfur, where the beast and the false prophet had been thrown. They will be tormented day and night for ever and ever.

{11} Then I saw a great white throne and him who was seated on it. Earth and sky fled from his presence, and there was no place for them. {12} And I saw the dead, great and small, standing before the throne, and books were opened. Another book was opened, which is the book of life. The dead were judged according to what they had done as recorded in the books. {13} The sea gave up the dead that were

in it, and death and Hades gave up the dead that were in them, and each person was judged according to what he had done. {14} Then death and Hades were thrown into the lake of fire. The lake of fire is the second death. {15} If anyone's name was not found written in the book of life, he was thrown into the lake of fire.

We come now to a chapter that has caused much controversy and debate throughout the ages due to different interpretations of the millennium. There were some who thought the millennial reign of Christ would begin when the calendar reached the year 2000. Many were wiser in their interpretation of Scripture. What is the thousand years mentioned in this chapter? Is it to be interpreted literally? Will Christ reign physically on the earth for a thousand years? Why should the devil be released after the thousand years? Why is there a first resurrection? What is it and who is included in this resurrection? Perhaps it will be helpful for you to read chapter 20 if you haven't already done so.

If we take this chapter literally, what we have is the imprisonment of Satan for a literal thousand years, or ten centuries. During this time, Christ will establish a physical government on earth. Only martyrs will be resurrected to reign with Christ during this period, after which Satan will be released to deceive the nations once again.

The above literal approach to chapter 20 is neither the most meaningful nor the most scriptural interpretation possible. I say that for the following reasons. First, this is a highly symbolic chapter in what is already a very symbolic book. What justification is there for taking a literal approach to such a symbolic chapter? We would not think of approaching Psalms (poetry) in such a fashion — why do it for Revelation 20? Second, a literal thousand-year reign is referred to only here in the whole Bible. It is not even mentioned in other parts of Scripture, both Old and New Testaments. Third, a literal approach to Revelation 20 does not fit the flow of the rest of Revelation. A good interpretation of this chapter should be consistent with the context of Revelation as a whole. Fourth, and perhaps most important, there is a more plausible interpretation that concurs not only with the immediate context of Revelation but also with the rest of the New Testament.

Here is the more plausible interpretation that is consistent with the rest of Scripture. Satan is bound for a symbolic thousand years during which his power and authority are limited, from the time of Christ's resurrection. Satan was defeated at the cross. Many became Christians in this period after the Church was born on the Day of Pentecost. At the conclusion of this symbolic thousand-year period, Satan is released from being bound so as to deceive the nations like never before. This begins the final Great Tribulation we have been studying, in which the beast and the false prophet emerge. When Christ comes again, He will slay the dragon together with the beast and throw them into the lake of fire. As can be seen, this interpretation is consistent with our study of the Revelation.

It is important to understand the word *bound*: *"He seized the dragon, that ancient serpent, who is the devil, or Satan, and bound him for a thousand years"* (verse 2). The devil is bound here in the sense that he is limited and restrained in his power and authority. His ability to deceive is severely curtailed, as evidenced by the many who have come into the Kingdom of God throughout the centuries. It is the same Greek word used in Matthew 12:29: *"Or again, how can anyone enter a strong man's house and carry off his possessions unless he first TIES UP the strong man? Then he can rob his house."* In this lesson of Jesus, the point is that Satan, the strong man, needs to be "bound" so that his captives can be set free into the Kingdom of God. The same scriptural principle is spelled out in John 12:31-32: *"Now is the time for judgment on this world; now the prince of this world will be driven out. But I, when I am lifted up from the earth, will draw all men to myself."* And again in Colossians 2:15: *"And having disarmed the powers and authorities, he made a public spectacle of them, triumphing over them by the cross."* That Satan is bound means he is confined, impeded and hindered in his work of deception. He lost his authority at the cross.

The angel in Revelation 20 bound the dragon in order *"to keep him from deceiving the nations anymore until the thousand years were ended"* (verse 3). The Gospel will be preached during this season of a symbolic thousand years (1,000 consists of three perfect tens multiplied: 10x10x10). During this time many will be martyred, since Satan is bound but not powerless. Remember that the devil was active even during the apostle Paul's ministry. But churches were planted everywhere across Asia Minor during the first century. What happens to the souls of martyrs during this long season? Revelation itself tells us that they are reigning with Christ in Heaven. This is the *"first resurrection"* of Revelation 20:4-5. Note that there is no indication that this first resurrection happens on earth or after the Second Coming. Indeed, it refers to the souls of the martyrs in Heaven.

"After that, he must be set free for a short time" (verse 3). At the close of the Church Age during the Great Tribulation we have the release of Satan from being bound. For a short time he will be given opportunity to deceive the nations. It is interesting that a "short time" is also mentioned in Revelation 12:12, in reference to the dragon: *"He is filled with fury, because he knows that his time is short."* What does he do in Revelation 20 after his release? The dragon *"will go out to deceive the nations in the four corners of the earth — Gog and Magog — to gather them for battle"* (verse 8). Gog is the chief prince of the land of Magog, representing the ends of the earth. In other words, he gathers world leaders from the globe for the Battle of Armageddon. Now everything makes sense within the contextual framework of Revelation itself. In chapter 19, we see judgment on the beast and the false prophet as they are thrown into the lake of sulfur. In chapter 20, we have judgment on the dragon, Satan himself, who is also thrown into the lake of fire: *"And the devil, who deceived them, was thrown into the lake of burning sulfur, where the beast and the false prophet had been thrown* (verse 10).

Now Judgment Day begins: *"Then I saw a great white throne and him who was seated on it. Earth and sky fled from his presence, and there was no place for them. And I saw the dead, great and small, standing before the throne, and books were opened. Another book was opened, which is the book of life. The dead were judged according to what they had done as recorded in the books"* (verses 11-12). The resurrection of the dead takes place: *"The sea gave up the dead that were in it, and death and Hades gave up the dead that were in them, and each person was judged according to what he had done"* (verse 13). All who have rejected Christ's salvation will be brought down by their own sins, as they have refused the righteousness of Christ. They will be judged according to their own righteousness. *"Then death and Hades were thrown into the lake of fire. The lake of fire is the second death. If anyone's name was not found written in the book of life, he was thrown into the lake of fire"* (verses 14-15). Only those who have accepted Christ's death on the cross on their behalf will escape the second death.

Conclusion

The devil deceives the world for a short time. It is only a very short duration from the standpoint of eternity. It is not worth following the dragon's deception, lest we be judged along with him. Life is more than just existing from day to day. Real life involves the choice to follow Christ in doing His will. God wants each of us to fulfil our destiny on earth. It is a once-in-a-lifetime deal! We all have a common destiny in Heaven which words cannot describe, but there is also a destiny on earth for the Christian. It involves doing what He has called you to do for His Kingdom, and being the unique person He wants you to be for His glory. Has He given you spiritual gifts? Use them. Do you have a mission? Walk in it. Does the Spirit of God live in you? Fellowship with Him, listen to His voice, and let Him empower you for the one short life you have on desert earth. Live it in the light of eternity.

Questions for Private Study and Discussion

1. What were the saints praising God for in the Hallelujah Chorus?

2. How can the Bride of Christ be ready for the Bridegroom?

3. What are the weaknesses of a literal approach to the millennial reign of Christ in chapter 20?

4. What are the strengths of the interpretation of chapter 20 offered by the author?

5. How might a Christian purposefully live in the light of eternity?

Chapter 20

VICTORY ASSURED

Revelation 21:

Then I saw a new heaven and a new earth, for the first heaven and the first earth had passed away, and there was no longer any sea. {2} I saw the Holy City, the new Jerusalem, coming down out of heaven from God, prepared as a bride beautifully dressed for her husband. {3} And I heard a loud voice from the throne saying, "Now the dwelling of God is with men, and he will live with them. They will be his people, and God himself will be with them and be their God. {4} He will wipe every tear from their eyes. There will be no more death or mourning or crying or pain, for the old order of things has passed away."

{5} He who was seated on the throne said, "I am making everything new!" Then he said, "Write this down, for these words are trustworthy and true."

{6} He said to me: "It is done. I am the Alpha and the Omega, the Beginning and the End. To him who is thirsty I will give to drink without cost from the spring of the water of life. {7} He who overcomes will inherit all this, and I will be his God and he will be my son. {8} But the cowardly, the unbelieving, the vile, the murderers, the sexually immoral, those who practice magic arts, the idolaters and all liars — their place will be in the fiery lake of burning sulfur. This is the second death."

{9} One of the seven angels who had the seven bowls full of the seven last plagues came and said to me, "Come, I will show you the bride, the wife of the Lamb." {10} And he carried me away in the Spirit to a mountain great and high, and showed me the Holy City, Jerusalem, coming down out of heaven from God. {11} It shone with the glory of God, and its brilliance was like that of a very precious jewel,

like a jasper, clear as crystal. {12} It had a great, high wall with twelve gates, and with twelve angels at the gates. On the gates were written the names of the twelve tribes of Israel. {13} There were three gates on the east, three on the north, three on the south and three on the west. {14} The wall of the city had twelve foundations, and on them were the names of the twelve apostles of the Lamb.

{15} The angel who talked with me had a measuring rod of gold to measure the city, its gates and its walls. {16} The city was laid out like a square, as long as it was wide. He measured the city with the rod and found it to be 12,000 stadia in length, and as wide and high as it is long. {17} He measured its wall and it was 144 cubits thick, by man's measurement, which the angel was using. {18} The wall was made of jasper, and the city of pure gold, as pure as glass. {19} The foundations of the city walls were decorated with every kind of precious stone. The first foundation was jasper, the second sapphire, the third chalcedony, the fourth emerald, {20} the fifth sardonyx, the sixth carnelian, the seventh chrysolite, the eighth beryl, the ninth topaz, the tenth chrysoprase, the eleventh jacinth, and the twelfth amethyst. {21} The twelve gates were twelve pearls, each gate made of a single pearl. The great street of the city was of pure gold, like transparent glass.

[22] I did not see a temple in the city, because the Lord God Almighty and the Lamb are its temple. {23} The city does not need the sun or the moon to shine on it, for the glory of God gives it light, and the Lamb is its lamp. {24} The nations will walk by its light, and the kings of the earth will bring their splendor into it. {25} On no day will its gates ever be shut, for there will be no night there. {26} The glory and honor of the nations will be brought into it. {27} Nothing impure will ever enter it, nor will anyone who does what is shameful or deceitful, but only those whose names are written in the Lamb's book of life.

Revelation 22:

Then the angel showed me the river of the water of life, as clear as crystal, flowing from the throne of God and of the Lamb {2} down the middle of the great street of the city. On each side of the river stood the tree of life, bearing twelve crops of fruit, yielding its fruit every month. And the leaves of the tree are for the healing of the nations. {3} No longer will there be any curse. The throne of God and of the Lamb will be in the city, and his servants will serve him. {4} They will see his face, and his name will be on their foreheads. {5} There will be no more night. They will not need the light of a lamp or the light of the sun, for the Lord God will give them light. And they will reign for ever and ever.

{6} The angel said to me, "These words are trustworthy and true. The Lord, the God of the spirits of the prophets, sent his angel to show his servants the things that must soon take place."

{7} "Behold, I am coming soon! Blessed is he who keeps the words of the prophecy in this book."

{8} I, John, am the one who heard and saw these things. And when I had heard and seen them, I fell down to worship at the feet of the angel who had been showing them to me. {9} But he said to me, "Do not do it! I am a fellow servant with you and with your brothers the prophets and of all who keep the words of this book. Worship God!"

{10} Then he told me, "Do not seal up the words of the prophecy of this book, because the time is near. {11} Let him who does wrong continue to do wrong; let him who is vile continue to be vile; let him who does right continue to do right; and let him who is holy continue to be holy."

{12} "Behold, I am coming soon! My reward is with me, and I will give to everyone according to what he has done. {13} I am the Alpha and the Omega, the First and the Last, the Beginning and the End.

{14} "Blessed are those who wash their robes, that they may have the right to the tree of life and may go through the gates into the city. {15} Outside are the dogs, those who practice magic arts, the sexually immoral, the murderers, the idolaters and everyone who loves and practices falsehood.

{16} "I, Jesus, have sent my angel to give you this testimony for the churches. I am the Root and the Offspring of David, and the bright Morning Star."

{17} *The Spirit and the bride say, "Come!" And let him who hears say, "Come!" Whoever is thirsty, let him come; and whoever wishes, let him take the free gift of the water of life.*
{18} *I warn everyone who hears the words of the prophecy of this book: If anyone adds anything to them, God will add to him the plagues described in this book.* [19] *And if anyone takes words away from this book of prophecy, God will take away from him his share in the tree of life and in the holy city, which are described in this book.*
{20} *He who testifies to these things says, "Yes, I am coming soon."* *Amen. Come, Lord Jesus.*
{21} *The grace of the Lord Jesus be with God's people. Amen.*

The New Jerusalem

These two final chapters are victory chapters. In chapter 21, we see that the new Jerusalem is in fact the Bride of Christ. *"I saw the Holy City, the new Jerusalem, coming down out of heaven from God, prepared as a bride beautifully dressed for her husband"* (verse 2). The new Jerusalem is the people of God, for she is *"the wife of the Lamb"* (verse 9). In New Testament ecclesiology, the Church is the Bride of Christ. At the same time it is the new city of God. Indeed the new Jerusalem represents both the dwelling and the dwellers. It is a city as well as its citizens. *"And he carried me away in the Spirit to a mountain great and high, and showed me the Holy City, Jerusalem, coming down out of heaven from God"* (verse 10).

The new Jerusalem is the magnificent dwelling of the people of God. It is our future home. Let's see what it's like. First, we are told that it is a cube. It measures 12,000 stadia on each side, meaning that it has a length of about 1,400 miles(2,200 kilometers) on each side. This is more than half the distance across America (more than twice the distance from Melbourne to Sydney). It is a symbol of perfection as 12,000 is 12x10x10x10. These round complete biblical numbers indicate that a literal interpretation should not be sought. The city has twelve gates, with one of the names of the tribes of Israel written on each gate. This represents the Old Testament people of God. *"The wall of the city had twelve foundations, and on them were the names of the twelve apostles of the Lamb"* (verse 14). This is the New Covenant people of God. All this confirms that the people of God are represented here, both those before Christ and those after Christ.

Second, the new Jerusalem is built with rare and exceptionally expensive material: pearl, gold and precious stones. The message is that even the splendor of Rome at the time of John cannot be compared. And for us living in the twenty-first century, no city on earth can compare with it. It is glorious, magnificent, "fantabulous," and beyond the description of words. Even this vision of John is limited by his three-dimensional experience on earth. God was communicating to John in a way that he could comprehend as a mortal living in the first century. Remember, all of us will have new resurrected bodies when Christ comes again. Jesus' resurrected body could walk through walls (cf John 20:26)!

Third, its gates will never be shut, symbolizing perfect security. There is absolute peace and a total absence of danger. *"He will wipe every tear from their eyes. There will be no more death or mourning or crying or pain, for the old order of things has passed away"* (verse 4). Interestingly, there is no temple is the new Jerusalem: *"I did not see a temple in the city, because the Lord God Almighty and the Lamb are its temple"* (verse 22).

We should not interpret these descriptions of the new city literally. Be assured, the real thing will blow us away. It will be a new Heaven and a new earth! The message given to us here is that the new Jerusalem is a city we want to be part of. It offers all that we will ever need or want: comfort, safety, security, peace, and even luxury (streets of gold)! It is a place of justice and integrity. There will be no more sickness and pain. Satan and his evil spirits are gone! The worship of God will truly be in spirit and in truth as the Lamb will be with us "in person." Yes, it is even worth dying for — a challenging message for those first-century hearers facing persecution, and for us.

Eternal Blessings

Chapter 22 tells us that the river of life is in the new city. So is the tree of life. *"Then the angel showed me the river of the water of life, as clear as crystal, flowing from the throne of God and of the Lamb"* (verse 1). This is a picture of eternal life and everlasting fulfilment. There will be no dissatisfaction, but joy and creativity will abound.

The final chapter also contains a blessing and a warning. First the blessing in verse 7: " *'Behold, I am coming soon! Blessed is he who keeps the words of the prophecy in this book.'* " The book of Revelation is to be understood and obeyed. If we keep His words, we will be blessed because we will be welcomed into the Holy City.

Now the warning in verses 18 and 19: *"I warn everyone who hears the words of the prophecy of this book: If anyone adds anything to them, God will add to him the plagues described in this book. And if anyone takes words away from this book of prophecy, God will take away from him his share in the tree of life and in the holy city, which are described in this book."* I trust that in my approach to the book I have not added to or taken away from the words of Jesus. None of us could bear the consequences.

Final Conclusion

As we come to the conclusion of this book, I hope you have enjoyed reading it as much as I have enjoyed writing it. I close with two phrases that Christ repeated seven times in His seven messages to the seven churches. *"He who overcomes..."* is the first of these exhortations. All seven churches had something to overcome in their situations. All of us too have something that needs overcoming in our Christian lives. Make it your determination to be an overcomer in this season of your life. Triumph over your circumstances regardless of what you might be facing. Build the seven qualities of an overcomer into your life: love, faithfulness, holiness, truth, watchfulness, "kingportunity" and zeal. Overcome so that you may receive the promise of victory.

The other often-repeated exhortation of Christ is: *"He who has an ear, let him hear what the Spirit says to the churches."* What is the Spirit of God saying to you today? What has He been saying to you as you read the chapters of this book? As the great hymn says it: "Trust and obey, for there's no other way to be happy in Jesus, but to trust and obey."

Finally, I close with a reminder of the golden spiritual season we are in here in the early years of the twenty-first century. It is the season of hope and harvest before the onset of the last Great Tribulation. It is the hour of the Gospel before the final beast rears its head. There are still many in the "10/40 Window" who have not heard the Good News even once. If there was ever a time to fulfill the Great Commission of Christ, it is now. Take your place in this global village, put on your armor, and join the eternal cause. *"He who testifies to these things says, 'Yes, I am coming soon.' Amen. Come, Lord Jesus. The grace of the Lord Jesus be with God's people. Amen."*

Questions for Private Study and Discussion

1. What are the three most important lessons you have learned from this book?

2. What has the Spirit said to you throughout the pages of this book?

3. How can you be a better overcomer in this season of your life?

4. How can you be more meaningfully involved in the Great Commission?

5. How has this book altered your view of the world?

6. How has your view of Jesus changed through your reading of this book?

7. What are your feelings now toward the book of Revelation? In light of your answers to the above questions, spend some time in worship of the risen Lamb.